# Democracy in Nigeria

*Thoughts and Selected Commentaries*

By

Anthony A. Akinola

**RB**
Rossendale Books

Published by Lulu Enterprises Inc.
3101 Hillsborough Street
Suite 210
Raleigh, NC 27607-5436
United States of America


First Edition Published in paperback 2013
Second Edition May 2015
Category: Political Essays
Copyright Anthony A. Akinola © 2013/2015

ISBN : 978-1-326-27086-5

# DEDICATION

To my children
Funmilayo, Bimbola and Tobi

# CONTENTS

# PREFACE AND ACKNOWLEDGEMENTS

There could be a time in the life of a nation when an historical episode changes the course of history for good; the annulment of a presidential election on 12 June 1993 may have done just that for Nigeria. That annulment of a "free and fair" election was an assault on decent sensibilities; coupled with their own culture of corruption, the military may have been badly discredited by it. Most Nigerians no longer see the military as the viable "alternative political party", even when contemporary political behaviour has hardly improved from what used to be the justifications for their intervention in politics.

The military handed over power to an elected government on 29 May 1999 and the democratic process powered by periodic elections has remained uninterrupted since then, the longest of such spells in a nation where political power has alternated between civilians and the military on several occasions. The military of old would have had cause to intervene in the democratic process and Nigerians of yesteryears would also have had cause to welcome such an intervention, whenever there is tension.

The culture of election rigging still defines the electoral process while corruption and corrupt practices have increased considerably. The presidency of Olusegun Obasanjo (1999 – 2007) would be remembered for a disgraceful feud between president and vice-president, not least because of the "suspicion" of an extra-constitutional "third term" agenda on the part of the former. That of the succeeding administration (2007 – 2010) was characterised by the impasse created by the incapacity of an ailing president, Umaru Musa Yar'Adua who subsequently died in office. The current presidency of Goodluck Jonathan (2010 to date) has been grappling with a state of insecurity since its inception.

"Continuity", however, is the platform from which to transform the "semi-democratic" state to a fully-fledged democracy where rules, regulations and principles are the norm. Democracy should be that system of government that brings benefit to all – not just a tiny minority of privileged politicians and officials. Democracy is not just about the processes of political governance, it is a culture that touches on inter-personal behaviour and relationships. The democrat is a man or woman of exemplary behaviour. The generality of Nigerians, including political writers and commentators, have a part to play in bringing about the appropriate democratic culture in our society. As one political writer, it has always been my aspiration to contribute to the development of democracy, its processes and culture... the very essence of my more than 30 years of writing for the public.

Be that as it may, the essays in this book were written over a period of time and many of them focus on important issues that are nevertheless inter-related or inter-connected. Inevitably there are repetitions here and there. Advocating an innovative idea for instance, could quite often be like engaging the deaf in a conversation. One just has to keep repeating things until the objective is achieved.

The decision to publish a few essays in book-form is to continue in engaging academia and the policy-making arena in discussions, in the assumption that the outcome would be beneficial to the Nigerian society. Such an assumption could not have arisen without the "assurances" from numerous individuals, known and unknown, who have had cause to commend my work. I have been hugely encouraged and I say "thank you" to all.

I am particularly grateful to the great scholars and intellectuals who have inspired me with their generous comments. They include the legendary Anthony Kirk-Greene( CMG, MBE) whose immense contributions to the understanding of Nigeria and its politics have continued to inform us. Professor Anthony Kirk-Greene spent valuable time reading through my manuscript and I am hugely flattered by his comments and foreword to this book; the great Charles W. Harris, my Professor of Political Science at Howard

University has continued to show immense interest in my work and family. Others include Professor Ladipo Adamolekun, Professor Gavin William, Dr Raufu Mustapha, Shehu Othman, Professor John Durodola, Dr Emmanuel Kaikai, Dr Phyllis Ferguson, Dr (Rev) Philip Kennedy who calls me "Prophet of Justice", Dr Shirley Ardener, Dr Edwin Madunagu and A B Assensoh , Professor Emeritus of African-American studies at Indiana University who enthusiastically shares my essays with friends and colleagues in the USA. And, of course, I can never forget my great friends who are no longer here with us, Dr Tajudeen Abdul-Raheem and Fidel Odum. May their souls rest in peace.

I am also grateful to those intelligent and good natured human beings who also show an interest in my work. They include Dr Biodun Adu, Rev. Oladunni Ogbede, Dr Remi Oyewumi, Dr Ayo Teriba, Anthony Aderiye, Taiwo Akinola, Mrs Dola Adejuyigbe, Gboyega Adewuyi, Gboyega Eko, Carl Zammit, Favour Momoh, Vincent Katende-Musungayi, Dr Sehinde Aruleba, Dr Olayinka Oduwaiye, Dr Vincent Bamigboye, Daniel Adams, Mrs Abimbola Solebo, Ben Akponasa, , Dr Gbenga Kazeem and James Boima Rogers who has shown exceptional interest and enthusiasm in this publication.

I am grateful to members of the larger Akinola family as represented by my senior brother, Colonel Emmanuel Akinola as well as to my wife, Shola Akinola (nee Adu) and children Funmi, Bimbola and Tobi. I am profoundly grateful to Joan and Meg Peacock who have always typed my scripts and have become integral members of my "Oxford family". Of course I am also grateful to Penny Rogers whose warm friendship with my family has been highly beneficial.

You may think you have written something great but could be disappointed and frustrated were the editor to have said "No" to its publication. In this regard I extend my gratitude to the editors of those great journals, magazines and newspapers who have published my essays. I say "thank you" to Dr Reuben Abati who is currently the spokesperson to the Nigerian President, Dr Goodluck Jonathan, as well as to Kunle Sanyaolu – both of The Guardian Newspaper of

11

Nigeria. Finally, I thank Chief Wole Olanipekun (OFR, SAN), who made a financial contribution of £500 towards putting my manuscript together. He has been such a thoughtful individual in many respects.

I must, however, state emphatically that all arguments in this book are exclusively mine, except where I have explicitly appropriated from others.

*Anthony Akinola*
*Oxford, June 2012*

# FOREWORD

To millions of Nigerians resident in their own country, along with several hundred thousands now living outside Nigeria, over the past twenty years the political journalism of Anthony Akinola has constituted a source of primary daily reading on Nigerian politics, progress and the problems of its democratic institutions. Today Akinola is recognised as a leading figure among the corps of journalists focusing on the politics of Nigeria. He has thus also played a notable part in enabling the progressive transfer of the writing and publication of books and articles on Nigeria's current politics away from expatriate leadership and more into the hands of local writers and publishers.

Born in 1946 in Ikere, Western Nigeria, Akinola was educated at the local St John's Primary School from 1952 to 1959 and then at Ikere's Annunciation Grammar School. On completion of his secondary education, he joined the Western Region's civil service in 1966, working in Ondo State. He resigned in 1979 in order to take up a place at Howard University in the USA, to read for a degree in political science. This was followed by his admission to Oxford University, where in 1986 he graduated in law. Since then his profession has been that of a journalist specialising in the politics of Nigeria, though living for most of the time in the UK, in Oxford. During these past 25 years Akinola has published over 500 essays in a number of Nigerian newspapers (principally <u>The Guardian</u> and <u>National Concord</u>), along with many articles on Nigerian political life written in the first place for his personal network <u>Yahoo! Mail</u>. Over the same period he published two books, <u>The Search for a Nigerian Political System</u> (1986) and <u>Rotational Presidency</u> (1996), as well as articles in international journals like <u>African Affairs</u>, <u>Modern African Studies</u>, <u>The Round Table</u> and the leading London-based, weekly magazine <u>West Africa</u> (established in 1917).

As I have followed Akinola's brilliant record of political journalism over the years, I have often asked myself what might be the main characteristic required in achieving such successful reportage. Three principal criteria can be identified. One, he must report and present his data accurately, fully and in a manner capable of attracting the attention of readers. Secondly, he should go beyond such straightforward presentation and in his commentaries start to analyse the data. Such analysis might perhaps include linking the new political aims and moves with the government's previous political reform initiatives and perhaps making an assessment of how far the current political strategy represents a genuinely fresh change in, say, democratisation or social engineering or maybe diplomatic relations. Thirdly, he should not be afraid to speculate, as it were, on the possible (and possibly unanticipated) outcome or spin-offs from the new legislation, for instance in such cases as riverain communities, exports, students, the unemployed or on selected industries, the communications network or national security. Unless a would-be modernising government takes care to look far enough ahead into the possible knock-on consequences of any new policy, it may easily experience the scornful disdain which greeted the UK government in 2012, when large parts of its legislation and budgetary decisions had to be publicly reversed as unworkable and hence withdrawn, thereby earning it the feckless nickname of a "U-turn government". It may be argued that to look beyond the legislation and publicly assess its consequences to a degree which the government has not done can emphatically be a rewarding opportunity for any political journalist who wants to show that he is truly on top of his job.

Let me add one more indicator of the intellectual respect Akinola has earned for himself among those who follow Nigerian politics. Recently, one of my former Nigerian students telephoned me to tell me about an unconfirmed report that the President's Office might be considering the drafting of a far-reaching plan to bring order into the somewhat oil-turmoil Delta State. He concluded his narrative with an expressive "Wow"! "So what next?" I enquired, "first of all we must see whether Akinola has anything to say on <u>Yahoo</u>" was the instant reply.

In conclusion, after many years of reading, enjoying and learning from Anthony Akinola's presentations of the political ups-and-downs of Nigeria's experience of progressive democracy, I do not hesitate in declaring that no library in Nigeria, nor any academic centres around the world which are interested in Nigeria's politics, can afford to be without a copy of Akinola's excellent <u>Democracy in Nigeria</u>. With such stimulating chapter titles as "Obasanjo and the Third Term Stigma", "Jonathan and the Zoning Controversy", "Ethnic Rivalry over Leadership", "The Monster of Corruption" and "Religion and Religiosity", Akinola is already assured of an enthusiastic readership for his book. It is a great pleasure, personal as well as professional, to have been invited by the author to write the Foreword to this book and I wish it all the success it so strongly deserves.

*A.H.M. KIRK-GREENE*
*Oxford, June 2012*

# INTRODUCTION

THE wish of every patriotic Nigerian and, indeed, all lovers of democracy worldwide, is that the handover of power by the military to a democratically elected government on May 29, 1999 marked the end of military intervention in Nigeria's politics. Rather than view the handover as a victory over the military, which it was not, the reasonable position is to examine what has made the military's intrusion the easiest of tasks and how not to make bad history repeat itself in the future.

The political history books are there to confirm that the coups, which ousted civilian governments in the past were popular and welcomed by public opinion. Although the military tended to extend their "tenure" through counter-coups or palace coups, the two points at which democratically elected governments were overthrown were in January 1966 and December 1983. The first occasion led to 13 years of military rule, the second to 16 years.

The first military coup received its immediate justification in the crisis that followed the massive rigging of elections in the old Western Region in 1965. The attempt by the leadership of the defunct Nigerian National Democratic Party (NNDP) to impose itself on the people of the West led to violence in which the killing of NNDP supporters and the burning of their houses was the order of the day. The inability or unwillingness of the Federal Government to restore order provided the platform for military intervention.

However, the crisis in the West was only the immediate cause of their intervention. The remote causes were deep rooted in the nature of Nigeria's heterogeneity and the politics of regionalism in the immediate post-independence era. The hotly disputed census of 1962-63 was viewed as an attempt by one axis of the country to impose its dominance over the other. Similarly for the disputed federal election of 1964 which more or less pitched the North against the South.

The attempted coup of January 1966 soon led Nigeria into a bloody civil war; as the coup planners were southern officers, mostly of Igbo origin and the victims, mostly, were venerated politicians and top military officers from the Northern Region. The coup makers' claim to patriotism could, therefore, not be sustained, not least because of the exclusion of Igbo politicians from the "cleansing" exercise.

During the subsequent years of military rule, there were two changes which would later make an impact on party politics: the creation of states and the replacement of parliamentary democracy with a presidential system of government patterned on the American presidential/congressional system.

The issue of state creation predated Nigeria's independence in 1960. There was agitation, sometimes violent, by the minority ethnic groups, especially those of the Middle Belt in the north and the Calabar-Ogoja-Rivers areas in the Eastern Region. The British colonial masters indicated, following the recommendations of the Willink Commission on the minority ethnic groups in 1958, that if new states were to be created, independence would have to be delayed for two years in order to allow the new states time to settle down. Because the nationalist politicians were in a hurry for independence, they could not agree to that idea.

After independence, because of the advantages of size in Nigeria's politics of regionalism, the only new region that was created by the politicians was the Mid-Western Region – more as a way of curtailing the influence of the Yoruba-dominated Western Region (out of which it was carved), whose authentic leadership was at loggerheads with the ruling coalition of the Northern People Congress (NPC) and the (Igbo dominated) National Convention of Nigerian Citizens (NCNC).

First under General Yakubu Gowon in 1967, later under Generals Murtala Muhammed, Ibrahim Babangida and Sani Abacha, the military split the former four regions into 36 states. Professor A.E. Afigbo, an eminent historian, described the contributions of Gowon's administration to the Nigerian federation in these flowing words: "...

it enabled the fundamental character of the Nigerian federation that is its multi-ethnic character, to emerge full and defiant, as well as naked, repulsive and challenging. Hitherto it had tended to be obscured by British-generated cleavages between mere geographical expressions such as between, first, North and South and then among North, East and West". (Federal Character and federalism in Nigeria (1989), p. 13)

The second major change, the introduction of presidential politics as a way of fostering greater political interaction among Nigeria's diverse groups, has also been significant. Because Nigeria's political parties were mostly ethnic-based, the "government" and "opposition" attributes of the erstwhile parliamentary system had merely resulted in one ethnic group allying itself against the other. Under the presidential system, whoever seeks to become president is required to win a majority of popular votes and meet certain requirements of geographical spread. The ugly feature of parliamentary politics as practised in Nigeria's First Republic (1960-66) was that the most powerful party, the NPC, did not even extend its membership to the southern regions and yet presided over the affairs of the federation.

The military handed over the reins of power to a democratically elected government on October 1, 1979. The election of the president was not without controversy. However, Alhaji Shehu Shagari, the flag bearer of the National Party of Nigeria (NPN) became Nigeria's first directly elected President.

The elected representatives in the National Assembly, it must be said, would appear to have deliberately refused to comprehend the rudiments of presidential politics. Under the guidance of their political parties, those who voted in support of bills sponsored by a member of another party were accused of "anti party" behaviour. The politics of "rub my back, I rub yours" was conducted in monetary terms.

The corruption that ensued in the Shagari era, especially among members of the NPN, was on a scale unprecedented in the history of Nigeria. In the face of general poverty in society, those at the top echelons of the party were busy flying their private jets all over the globe, conducting one business after another. General Olusegun Obasanjo who handed over power to Shagari summed up the extravagance of the NPN-controlled executive when, in a keynote address, he hinted that the Shagari administration had spent over N50 billion -a colossal sum in those days— in less than four years with nothing to show for it.

The demise of the Second Republic (1979-83) came with the politics of re-election. Alhaji Shehu Shagari, whose performance in office had been unimpressive, was re-elected in what his supporters celebrated as a "landslide" victory. However, the NPN's incursion into opposition territory was soon to spark a major crisis, especially in Ondo State where the NPN governor-elect had to flee the state in the face of violence directed against NPN supporters. The courts of law assumed the role of electoral officials as they overturned one victory after the other.

The overthrow of the Epicurean politicians was greeted with nationwide jubilation, not least among students, journalists and ordinary Nigerians. It must be said that members of opposition parties had actually called on the military opportunists to overthrow the Shagari government, not knowing that the hurricane would sweep away all democratic institutions nationwide.

What followed the Shagari presidency was 16 years of military rule, featuring such corrupt dictators as Ibrahim Babangida and Sani Abacha. Their misrule, and annulment of a presidential election on June 12, 1993, which need not be dwelt upon here, should provide Nigerians with a lesson in the importance of "self-rule" as opposed to military dictatorship.

Now that democracy is back, the politicians must ensure that it works. There are two sides to a stable democracy; the constitutional aspect, which provides the rules and nature of power relations in written form (except in Britain where the constitution is unwritten) and the human factor, which has to do with the behaviour of political elites and their supporters. Both the constitutional framework and the elements of

19

human behaviour must be appropriate and complementary for democracy to survive in any given society.

The constitutional framework agreed to by Nigeria's founding fathers is the federal one. When the first military ruler, Major-General J.T.U Aguiyi-Ironsi, reversed it to install a unitary system via the Unification Decree No. 34 on May 24, 1966, it sparked off an immediate anti-Igbo "revolt" in the North where his action was suspected to be an attempt to impose his own group's domination over the rest of Nigeria and especially over the North, which was behind the other regions in Western education and commerce. Lt-Col Yakubu Gowon (as he then was) returned the nation to the federal status quo following the counter-coup of July 29, 1966.

However, many years of military rule have eroded the tradition of federalism in Nigeria. Today Nigeria is federal only in name. Many informed commentators on Nigerian politics have argued vociferously for Nigeria to return to a true federalism. The issue of Sharia, which has disturbing implicit dangers for the nation's fragile democracy, is a federal issue, which should be resolved constitutionally or by legal interpretation in the courts of law, instead of resort to violence. Most of the ideas that are today incorporated into the constitutions and political arrangements of developing nations emerged from constitutional or legal resolution of issues that were once contested somewhere else in the past.

Politicians do not have to live in perpetual fear of the military. They must make innovative and far-reaching decisions on the organisation of state and society and carry the people along with them. What they must not do is continue with the irresponsibility of yesteryear.

The culture of corruption, political intolerance and the arrogance of power have not helped the cause of democracy anywhere in the world. One salutary development today is the seeming consensus among Nigerians that democracy, even as crude as it still is in their society, is more acceptable than the most benevolent of dictatorships. In the not-too-distant past, they would have called upon the military to

20

overthrow a democratically -elected government that was grappling with problems of democracy and nation-building. That they have not done so in spite of current difficulties suggest they have learnt a few lessons from many years of corrupt and purposeless authoritarian rule. Democracy may have come to stay in Nigeria.

# PART 1

## ETHNIC RIVALRY OVER LEADERSHIP

**SYNOPSIS**

*Nigeria is multi-ethnic; its main features include the existence of major ethnic groups each territorially exclusive and larger than many nations of the world. Languages vary with the groups, and so also do culture and religious practices. Particularly because of these features of the Nigerian state, political leadership has tended to be contended along regional sentiments and loyalties, with devastating consequences. The arguments here favour the rotation of the presidency between defined ethno-sectional constituencies. Many Nigerians accept that is the only route to peace and stability in their nation.*

## The legacy of June 12

The significance of June 12 is not in the presidential election of June 12 1993; the significance is in the crisis that greeted its annulment. That crisis would have achieved a purpose if it resulted in a permanent end to military intrusion in politics.

The authors of the political arrangement that gave birth to what has now become a historic election did not intend the election of June 12 1993 to lead to democracy. Had Chief Moshood Abiola, its presumed winner, been allowed to lead a government, such a government would probably have been overthrown in a matter of months without provoking the type of anger generated by that annulment.

The legendary ambition of General Sani Abacha comes to mind in arguing this thesis. Abacha, Abiola and General Ibrahim Babangida who annulled the presidential election of June 12 1993, were opportunistic friends. It is doubtful if Chief Abiola would have had the wisdom or courage to retire General Abacha from the military. If that had been the case he would have been cohabiting with a dangerous political "cobra". With the type of reckless ambition exhibited by Abacha when he overthrew the Interim Government led by Chief Ernest Shonekan in November 1993 until his own death in June 1998, it can hardly be over exaggerated that Abacha would have chosen an occasion to put an end to a putative government led by Moshood Abiola.

The overthrow of such a government would possibly have been taken as an occurrence we have become accustomed to in Nigerian politics. The emotion generated by the annulment of the June 12 election, the emotion that a Yoruba man had been denied the presidency, would not have been there. There would have been quick references to the fact that the Shehu Shagari-led democratic government of 1979-1983 was overthrown by an officer from his own ethnic region. Sympathy for a possible overthrow of a Moshood Abiola-led government would have been subdued if its performance were equally as dismal as that of Shehu Shagari and his National Party of Nigeria (NPN). The fact of no previous experience in governmental politics – forget about this personal generosity thing which has nothing to do with running an effective government – suggests that Abiola's "political teething" problems might have been unsurprisingly evident.

Talking about the June 12 1993 presidential election itself, the one thing that Nigerians have continued to "celebrate" about it was that ethnicity and religion played little or no part in their voting decisions. As enthusiastic as one has always been in matters of our politics, it took quite a number of enquiries to be able to have an insight into what kind of personality Alhaji Bashir Tofa, the opponent of Bashorun MKO Abiola in that election, was. Bashorun Abiola who was once hated by members of his immediate Yoruba constituency for being "more northern than the northerner" could not have had an easier "prey" to contest against. All told, the Alhaji Bashir Tofa of 1993 was a "nobody" politically and Nigerians deserve commendation for acknowledging that in their non-fully declared votes. The role played by ethnicity and religion in the presidential election of 2011 would suggest there was naivety in our assumption that June 12 1993would have ended the influence of these cleavages.

However, there is little or no doubt that the presidential election of June 12 1993 was relatively free and fair. It was a lot easier to manage, not least because of fewer candidates and a restricted number of participating political parties. However, the structure of an imposed two-party arrangement would probably not have survived the test of time. The two manufactured political parties – the Social Democratic Party (SDP) and the National Republican Convention (NRC) – might have eventually collapsed, giving birth to the type of unruly political parties that we have today. The truth of the matter is that a two-party system does not come about because we wish it; there are factors which help the culture and sustenance of the two-party system.

Be that as it may, the post annulment crisis that greeted the deserved death of the two political parties may have been proving to be the War of Independence Nigerians needed to fight against military involvement in governmental politics. Had we not had the fight at the time we did, the relevance of the military in politics might still be very strong today. Many would have thought their intervention was necessary in quite a number of crisis situations – the Sharia-induced crisis of 2000, the impasse created by the illness of the late President Umaru Yar'Adua in 2009/2010 and the post-election violence in April 2011, which claimed many lives. That we no longer encourage their intrusion and that they themselves no longer flaunt their ambition, would seem to have been our consensus that politicians are entitled to learn from their own mistakes. If that matured thinking is what we have taken from the annulment crisis, then June 12 should be regarded as a fulfillment of immense proportions.

*Daily Trust, 13 June 2011*

# The Presidency in context

PRESIDENTIALISM thrives on the principle of Separation of Powers. The principle, with its checks and balances, emphasizes the division of responsibilities between three arms of government - Executive, Legislative and Judicial. Of the three arms of government, the Executive is undoubtedly the most feasible and powerful. It is a "one-man office", with the occupant otherwise known as "President", doubling as Head of State and Head of Government. The President, therefore, personifies the state; whatever he or she does has implications beyond the national boundaries. The President is "first without equals".

The presidential system of government contrasts the parliamentary alternative, not least because political power is fused in the latter. Members of the Executive are drawn from the political party (or political parties) with the majority of seats in the Legislature. Whereas, in theory, an independent candidate can be President by election, such a feat is impossible in a parliamentary system of government. The Prime Minister, who is first and foremost a member of parliament, heads the government. The Prime Minister owes his or her position to colleagues, making the PM "first among equals".

Nigeria has had the luxury of experiencing both the parliamentary and presidential systems of government. The country inherited parliamentarism from the British colonialists but currently operates a presidential system patterned on the American Constitution. The choice of presidentialism became necessary because of the chaos engendered in the practice of parliamentarism in a severely divided nation. Not least because the early political parties were ethnically-based and ethnically-informed, it was assumed that the presidential alternative would create a more interwoven process.

That expectation might have been achieved somehow, not least because when presidentialism replaced parliamentarism in 1979, politicians with aspirations for the presidency have seen the need to cultivate friendship and political support beyond the divides. This was scarcely the case in the First Republic, which was terminated by a military coup d'état in January 1966. During that era the leadership of Nigeria's then most powerful party, the Northern People's Congress (NPC) did not seek direct political support from the southern regions. What characterized the politics of the First Republic was a culture of party alliances, unstable as they were, which sought co-operation among themselves in order to be able to challenge for power at the centre.

Such alliances may not be the most realistic approach in the presidential context where the strength of a political party determines its capability to win a major election. Post-electoral coalitions scarcely determine the course of the presidency. The defunct National Party of Nigeria (NPN) captured the essence of presidentialism and seemed more realistic than its then rivals in the understanding of the nature of the Nigerian political terrain.

The idea of "zoning", or a policy of alternating the presidency between regions, came with the formation of the NPN in 1978. The idea emanated from the realization that political leadership was a divisive issue. The idea worked for the NPN, as it also seems to have worked for today's ruling People's Democratic Party (PDP), in the sense that both parties have arguably been the only truly national political parties in the history of Nigerian democracy. Unlike rival political parties, both the NPN and PDP cut across the divides.

However, an idea that seems capable of stabilizing an otherwise chaotic situation should not be restricted to a political party. What is honestly accepted to be a national problem should be addressed in a national constitution. The politics of succession in the aftermath of President Umaru Musa Yar'Adua's death in 2010, highlights the apparent conflict in a political party wanting to implement an idea, which the national constitution did not endorse. Goodluck Jonathan, who succeeded Yar'Adua as President, might not have been in a position to seek the presidency in the 2011 presidential election, had the principle of alternating the presidency between regions been in the provision of the national constitution.

The controversy, which the candidacy of Goodluck Jonathan generated, argues the case for introducing the principle in the national constitution. Even when the incapacity of President Yar'Adua had become apparent, there were those who would deny it because of the fear that the presidency would shift to another region of the Nigerian federation. The PDP might still have been able to insist on the sanctity of its philosophy, oblivious of a constitutional crisis, had Jonathan not been a member of a geo-political constituency that could make the nation pay for it. There was the fear that members of his immediate ethnic constituency could disrupt oil production out of anger, if he was denied the opportunity to run for office.

The 2011 presidential election itself was characterized by all sorts of sentiments, which had nothing to do with the ability of contestants to lead. For instance, in the North, such sentiments were expressed in violence. It can only be through a constitutional device that such sentiments can be contained in the Nigerian practice of democracy.

The prediction or suggestion that Nigeria could disintegrate by 2015 can be doused, only by Nigerians themselves. The strength of a nation could be in the honest understanding of what its weaknesses are. The warnings have recurred throughout Nigerian history, since independence in 1960, that the quest for leadership has been the major issue that pitches one group against another. The year 2015 promises so much in this regard.

*The Guardian 20 April 2012*

# Rotational presidency can stabilize Nigeria

WHEN children of different mothers quarrel over their patrimony, it is only an who says that peace in the family is not what matters most. Nigeria is one larger "polygamous" setting whose fratricidal feuds over the years provide useful lessons for those who care to learn from history.

The major feuds in the Nigerian polity since independence in 1960 have been mainly over leadership. Be it the Civil War of 1967-70 or the Gideon Orkar-led attempted coup of April 1990, or the crisis we now simply refer to as "June 12", it has been demonstrated in the course of our existence as an independent nation that the leadership question is indeed the national question.

To the credit of Nigerians, the enormity of the leadership question appears to have been understood. The arrangement by the ruling People's Democratic Party (PDP) to rotate the presidency between the South and North is an acknowledgement of the existence of a most disturbing national problem, and an effort to provide a practical solution to it. The PDP approach would appear to have reasonably stabilised Nigeria in the last 10 years, as the fear of "ethnic hegemony" would appear not to have been as pronounced as it once was.

However, we do not have "rotational presidency" yet. The principle is yet to be accommodated in the national Constitution where its "nitty gritty" can be spelt out. The confusion generated by the health of President Umaru Musa Yar'Adua, if anything, amplifies the need to do so without any further delay.

A Constitution or political arrangement must accommodate the emotions and sentiments of those it is designed to serve if its usefulness is to survive the test of time. One has said it before, and one is repeating it here, that the success of the American constitution is the acknowledgement by America's founding fathers that the problem of cleavage can only be resolved by addressing it. Their pragmatic decision to introduce a bicameral legislature was one "scientific" approach to addressing the fears of smaller states about the dominance of larger ones. Hence the American states, irrespective of their sizes and populations, were accorded equal representation in the Senate. Today, the State of Wyoming with a population barely over one million people enjoys equal representation as California whose population is well over 30 million. However, representation in the House was based on population. We in Nigeria have merely devalued the essence of a bicameral legislature by creating states that are more or less of equal size.

Cleavages, be they those of ethnicity and religion, do not disappear as we naively assume they will. The sad prediction here is that our cleavages may eventually destroy our aspiration of one Nigerian nation if we do not learn how to manage them effectively. We sadly do not appear to be an innovative people, hence our inability to provide "homegrown" solutions to problems that are uniquely ours. Had the Americans been confronted with our type of ethnological realities and chose to have rotational presidency, all of us would today have been singing the praises of the idea. The Americans, by their Constitution of 1787, introduced into the world of politics the concepts of bicameralism, federalism, presidential/congressional system and limited government. They charted a course for democracy.

Critics of rotational presidency talk of having the "best candidate" for the job, even when they know that such a so-called best candidate always comes from a dominant regional grouping. There are "best candidates" in every region of the Nigerian federation, seeking an opportunity to bring their leadership qualities to bear on all of us. The good thing about our society today, as opposed to those days of omniscient military rule, is that we have come to accept democracy as irreplaceable and individuals have the opportunity to demonstrate their preparedness for upward mobility through their performances at other tiers of political governance.

Rotational presidency should be entrenched in our Constitution, not least because of its potential to stabilise our otherwise severely divided society. This writer submitted a detailed memorandum on this subject to the Political Bureau instituted by the government of General Ibrahim Babangida in 1986. Interestingly, a committee of intelligent,

29

experienced and well-meaning Nigerians - The Patriots - articulated a similar proposal in the year 2000. The fact that we have ever since remained loyal to our viewpoint suggests honesty and conviction on our part.

We sadly have too many so-called opinion leaders in our society who say one thing today and another tomorrow. Sadly, because these so-called opinion leaders have been "former this" or "former that", they get the attention they hardly deserve. Some pretend to be speaking for all of us, even when what they seek to protect is their selfish or group interests.

Rotational presidency is not "undemocratic". A nation is qualified to be called a democracy if it respects agreed rules and procedures. Switzerland, a small nation though it is, has cleavage problems quite similar to ours. It operates a system of "collective presidency" in which leadership is rotated annually. Switzerland is one of the world's most democratic and stable nations.

The country enjoys such stability that our corrupt politicians find it the safest place for their stolen monies! Rotational presidency, one argues, will regulate the party system beyond our wildest imaginations. The reason we have so many purposeless political parties is because of "noise makers" who require platforms for their indulgences. One strongly believes we could actually have principled political parties once their "ethnic hobs" have been removed. Given the realities of our society, only a system of rotational presidency will bring this about.

Rotational presidency, in this writer's view, complements and enhances the principle of federalism. Those who say it would divide Nigeria might as well call for a unitary system of government and, therefore, the scrapping of the states!

*The Guardian, 31 December 2009*

# Presidency Is The Issue

The Great Nnmadi Azikiwe had his own special "political anthem" when campaigning in the old western region populated by the Yoruba. He often sang in Yoruba to the applause of his audience, a song saying we should build our house on a rock because the one built on sand gets easily washed away.

The history book tells us of great nations that have collapsed because many fundamentals were swept under the carpet . Had the defunct Soviet Union followed the path of the United States of America by putting appropriate democratic structures in place, rather than indulging in many decades of sloganeering, it might have survived until today. Nigeria can only learn from the history of others if its own is not to be continuation in the chapter of failed nations.

There are things to admire in American political history ,not least the pragmatic solutions the founding fathers offered to controversial issues when the nation was transforming from a confederacy to a federal union in the latter part of the 18th century. The introduction of a bicameral legislature to reconcile the fears of smaller states about the dominance of larger ones in act of exceptional ingenuity. the device might have looked comical at some stage but share commitment by a succession of disciplined and purposeful politicians has seen the arrangement survive more than two centuries of political practice.

It is not likely one would find a reference to political parties in the American Constitution, not least because the institution of political parties was one development that came afterwards. Today's Democratic and Republican parties are mere electoral machines, parties that hold different meaning to different people in the fifty states of the federation. The American political parties are not ideological in the same context that most European political parties are.

When it is said that the American elected politician does not vote strictly along the party lines it is principally because of the diversity of interest in the American society. If, for instance, one is from a tobacco growing state, he or she has no business supporting a bill proposing a ban on smoking in public places. The line between the Republican party and the Democratic party is very thin, hence their peaceful co-existence over the years. The Nigerian political parties, on the other hand, have yet to develop a character, as politicians still display the type of loyalty that makes prostitutes look like devoted housewives.

Contemporary America may be as heterogeneous as Nigeria but it is not an ethnically-divided society. As Nigeria is approaching an election year the reality of the society is fast blowing onto the surface. The noise has been about the next president coming from the South-South, the South-East or the North. It would be dishonest or ill-informed to assume the presidency is not an issue in Nigerian politics. It is indeed a big issue and will remain so until it is boldly addressed in a new Constitution. Contentions over leadership have been responsible for the Civil War of 1967-70 and many other crises experienced in recent years. The writer once said in an article, and he is repeating it here, that the single institution that can keep Nigeria together or tear it apart is that of the presidency.

The main reason why groups scramble for the presidency in our type of society is not because of the expectation that the political leader or president will favour his or her own group over and above others. Groups want the presidency for psychological reasons. - be it the psychology of domination, or that of not wanting to be subservient. The renowned constitutional lawyer, Professor Ben Nwabueze, once said emphatically that the quest for a Nigerian president of Igbo origin was not an aspiration that could be abandoned simply because there was one president from somewhere else who was developing Igbo roads or even transforming every Igbo citizen into a millionaire. It is in the nature of ethnic politics that one group measures its own progress in society against the successes of rival groups.

The Yoruba did not consider the candidacy of General Olusegun Obasanjo favourably in 1999, not least because his only challenger in the then presidential election was a preferred kinsman. He won the presidency outside of Yoruba constituency. However, when Obasanjo sought re-election in 2003 and had no-Yoruba contenders as his opponents he won massively in his ethnic constituency. The Yoruba-dominated Alliance for Democracy (AD) tactically refused to present its own presidential candidate in order to boost Obasanjo's ethnic support. The facts of our politics are there for all to see

Issues can only be resolved when they are addressed. The issue of state creation was once a crippling phenomenon in Nigerian politics. Political parties were formed to actualise groups aspirations for separate states or regions. The United Middle Belt Congress (UMBC) and the United Independence Party (UNIP) were examples of such one-issue oriented political parties of the First Republic. In fact, agitation for state creation provoked large scale violence in some areas of the Nigerian Federation. Successive military governments did well to address this one-disturbing issue and the Nigerian Federation is all the better for it today.

Nations differ from one another and so also does the temperament of their occupants. There could not have been a state of California with a population of 35.9 million existing alongside a tiny Wyoming of 506.5 thousand in our own society. What about the possible agitation by governorship and senatorial aspirants for our own California to be split into 10 or more states in order to accommodate their ambitions? With states tending towards equal sizes, can we honestly say  today that bicameral legislature hold the same relevance and significance for us as it does for the nation that invented it? It serves no useful purpose for us to want to do things the way Americans do if out circumstance call for something different.

The argument that a potential president should be intelligent, competent and patriotic cannot, in any way, be faulted. However, those with such qualities can be found in all the geo-political zones of the Nigerian federation. The time will come, and it may not be long, when we see conventional wisdom in a remodelled presidency that is made up of an elected leader from each of the geo-political zones. The position of president who combines the functions of Head of State with that of the Chairmanship of the Collegiate can be based on rotation.

Because of the belief that Nigeria is one important nation of the world whose political leader deserves a face, the preferred model here is one in which a zone hold on to the position of Head of State and therefore, the title of President for duration of a single term of whatever number of year the Constitution prescribes. The members of the Collegiate will be entitled to seek re-election. When we have done this we will have build our nation and its democracy on a rocky foundation.

*The Guardian, 20 June 2006.*

# Democracy and structures of governance

This essay is a comment on the interesting article by Professor Emmanuel Anosike in <u>The Guardian</u> of 23 August 2006. The article, entitled "The clamour for a sectional president", assumes that a possible adoption of a system of rotational presidency in Nigeria is a departure from the democracy of the advanced, democratic nations of the western world which we seek to copy. I disagree.

I begin my comment by summarising democracy as an idea which, among other things, is about respect for the rule of law, free and fair elections and the freedom of the individual within the confines of the law. A nation may choose to put in place political structures which accord with its realities, what makes such a nation democratic or not is the extent to which the principles of democracy are upheld in the society. Structures of political governance differ and vary in western countries. What *we* lack, and must seek to learn, is the primacy they accord to the principles of their chosen political systems.

Great Britain, the United States of America, France and Switzerland are all western nations whose political systems and mode of electing national leaders vary from one to the other. Britain operates what is universally known as the Westminster model of parliamentary democracy; the British Prime Minister is first and foremost a Member of Parliament representing his or her local constituency. The current British Prime Minister, Mr Tony Blair, has indicated his intention to quit office in 2007 and his successor will be determined exclusively by Members of Parliament elected under the platform of his Labour Party. Britain has no written constitution, its practices derive from tradition, customs and usages. The King or Queen is the British Head of State, the Government is his or hers and the Opposition is expected to be loyal.

The United States of America has the oldest written constitution in the world. The President of the USA is elected nationally, sharing power with the executive and legislative arms of government. The American nation consists of autonomous states and national unity is cemented in a bicameral legislature. The American culture emphasises the equality of human beings, a fact that is underlined in a constitutional provision which says "No American citizen shall bear a title of nobility".

France operates a system of presidential/parliamentary democracy. The President is elected nationally, while there is a prime minister who superintends the affairs of parliament. Switzerland, on the other hand, premises its unity and stability on a system of "collective presidency" in which the position of president is rotated annually. The Swiss opted for this system after many years of instability, not least because it is one nation divided by cleavages that are not even as severe as those that divide us in Nigeria.

If we demarcate Nigeria into geo-political zones or presidential constituencies for the purpose of rotating the presidency – common sense and political reality suggest we should – the President elected under such a system cannot be a "sectional president". The President cannot be sectional because the political arrangement we borrowed from the United States of America enjoins the President to share power with elected senators and representatives who represent various constituencies in our nation. There is also the judicial arm of government with its own powers over constitutional issues. The "third term" debacle should remind all of us that the president cannot always have its way with determined ethnic politicians that we have in Nigeria by virtue of our natural divisions. A military dictator can choose to be sectional but an elected president can only do so at the risk of impeachment.

The institution of the presidency can be designed with the unity and stability of our nation as the primary and most important consideration. We tend to assume that it is the fault of the President if rain does not fall in our cities, towns and villages. There are tiers of government, other than federal, which should be held responsible for other constitutional roles. Experiences in Europe and America suggest that local government councils impact more on development than central governments which are more or less the arena for policy formulation. One would like to see our local government councils strengthened and empowered over the years so they can perform the roles and responsibilities of developing cities, towns and villages. The third tier of government should be manned by competent men and women who are determined to impact on their local communities and not the current bunch of incompetent politicians.

Groups want the presidency for psychological reasons and with party conventions and national elections approaching, the realities of our inter-ethnic relations have again come to the fore. Governor Ahmed Yerima of Zamfara state, a presidential hopeful under the platform of the All Nigeria Peoples Party (ANPP), has warned that it would be a mistake for the ruling Peoples Democratic Party (PDP) to pick its presidential candidate outside the North (The Guardian, 27 November). There is no doubt that the PDP is the party to beat in the forthcoming presidential election, not least because it is the largest and most cohesive party with resources of state power at its disposal. What Governor Yerima was saying was that with the North determined to produce the next President of the Nigerian Federation, support for the PDP in the region could erode if its presidential candidate were to come from somewhere else. With Yoruba politicians seemingly uninterested in the presidential ticket, not least because the current president is a member of their group, the logic and sentiment in our nation's presidential politics is there for all to see.

However, there is one element in the emerging Nigerian political behaviour which gives much hope for the future. Nigerians have demonstrated over the years their enthusiasm for electing a president regardless of the ethnic origins of the presidential candidates, and such a factor works favourably for a system of rotational presidency. The minority ethnic groups had always voted even when the presidential candidates were from the majority ethnic groups. In 1999 when the presidential contest pitched one Yoruba against another, there was enthusiastic voting all over the country. One should not be surprised if the highest voting percentage were to be recorded among the Yoruba in 2007 because every Nigerian is interested in who their president is.

*The Guardian 11,December 2006*

# Ethnicity as a permanent phenomenon

Ethnicity is one phenomenon we are not going to be able to wish away, no matter how much we try. Accepting ethnicity as a reality to be confronted is the way forward to achieving a stable, democratic nation. The magnitude of the problem posed by ethnicity in our society emanates from its centralised nature. While it is perhaps inconceivable that a nation like the United States of America would disintegrate because of its ethnic components, the same can hardly be said about Nigeria. The ethnic population in America is dispersed, and that explains one major difference between that nation and ours.

There is a lot to learn from the history of nations like Great Britain and Belgium, for instance, that could help in dispatching our naivety about ethnicity as one phenomenon. Many naively assume it is a matter of time for ethnicity to be a thing of the past. The danger with such an assumption is that a problem that deserves a pragmatic solution is abandoned to wishful thinking.

Great Britain, just like the Nigerian nation it created, emerged as a "merger" of nationalities. The merger began with the unification of England and Wales through the Act of Union in 1536 and concluded with that between England and Scotland in 1707. Both England and Scotland had shared the same monarch since the "Union of the Crown" in 1603 "when King James inherited the throne from his double first cousin Queen Elizabeth I". Great Britain was governed as a unitary state until recently, 1997 to be precise, when parliaments were created for Scotland and Wales with substantial devolution of power from Westminster, making Great Britain a quasi-federal nation. If ethnicity has been a temporary phenomenon, one would have assumed that more than three hundred years of union would have seen it disappear!

Belgium is another historic nation - historic in the sense that it was one of the European powers that colonised Africa - that has transformed from being a unitary state to a federal union. Belgium itself became independent in 1830, and had been a unitary state until 1970 when a series of reforms which continued until 2001, brought about new changes. Political power is shared between communities, regions (The Flemish, the French and the German-speaking groups) and the Federal State. "$ the power to make decisions is no longer the exclusive preserve of the federal government and the federal parliament. The leadership of the country is now in the hands of various partners, who independently exercise their authority within their domains."

We had, in the past, said quite a few things about Switzerland, a country whose political system is acknowledged today as "the world's most stable democratic system, offering a maximum of participation to citizens". The political history of Switzerland was turbulent indeed, significantly noted for revolts, a revolution in 1798 and a civil war in 1847. The word "putsch" for a violent overthrow of government is one vocabulary Switzerland gave to the world. This rather small country, as one once highlighted in an article, has the second oldest written constitution in the world. Its political arrangement, especially the collegiate executive with a rotating presidency every year, is the adaptation of the American presidential system to Switzerland's own peculiarities.

The United States of America, a nation with the first ever written constitution in the world, had to resolve a series of contentious issues in transforming from a confederacy of 13 independent states into a federal union in 1787. The founding fathers were confronted with the task of reassuring smaller states that they would benefit in a union consisting of larger ones, and they achieved this by instituting a bi-camera legislature. Today, if one must indulge in repetitive insistence on a position, the state of California with well over 30 million people, is represented in the Senate by two Senators, just as is the State of Wyoming or that of Alaska which have a little over a million inhabitants. The other major controversy concerned disputes over the status of slaves between the industrial North and the mainly agricultural South - the latter had a large population of slaves. The controversy was resolved by a decision to count each slave as three-fifths of a person for the purposes of taxation and representation. The resolution of the then contentious issues was hailed as "The Great Compromise" or "The Connecticut Compromise".

Americans may now tout that nation as the land of free peoples, but was this always the case? There is a journey every great nation must travel; Nigeria cannot be an exemption, no matter how hard we pretend to be what we are not. We must, however, not despair because ours is one great nation in the making. Those who have enthusiastically predicted the disintegration of our nation insult our collective wisdom and ability to rise to the challenges of history. Their prediction of doom is not borne out of superior intellectual reasoning, but guesswork informed by a recurring history of leadership controversy known to every Tom, Dick and Harry. However, they dare us to prove their prediction wrong. They do this by actually putting a date on when it would manifest, and it is not as if there are not Nigerians enthusiastically wishing for a doomsday! Even those who should be protecting a heritage are behaving madly!

Maybe there is a time in the life of a nation when "a voice from the wilderness" deserves to be heeded! One has been arguing rather furiously as if one's life depends on it, that a rotational presidency is the appropriate leadership arrangement for our type of society. One has also been arguing that no nation of the world has a magic solution, otherwise there would have been one model of democracy for all to embrace. Just as Switzerland has done to great advantage, it is hereby restated that the presidency of the Federal Republic of Nigeria would need to be adapted to the realities of our nation. The sentiments of our people, not least the disturbing disputes within the ranks of the ruling People's Democratic Party endorse this proposal.

*The Guardian, 03November 2010*

# Society and systems of governance

The two great systems of political governance known to the world of democracy, the parliamentary and the presidential, have been embraced by Nigeria since independence in 1960.

More than most democratic or semi-democratic nations, Nigerians are well-placed to assess the two political systems vis-à-vis the priority of their society. The impact the presidential system of government is capable of having on a society that is as heterogeneous as ours may not necessarily be the same as the parliamentary alternative.

The Westminster-type parliamentary system is a product of historical evolution while the American presidential system came into being following the Connecticut Convention of 1787. The presidential constitution itself was more or less the endorsement of views canvassed by Alexander Hamilton, James Madison and John Jay. Anyone who has read the *Federalist Papers* will appreciate the great thinking that went into every element of the American Constitution.

Although the American Constitution has been amended several times since its adoption, the great tribute to the purposefulness of the American people is in the fact that there has been no other constitutional convention since the Connecticut one. The American Constitution provides two methods of amendment. The first method is for a Bill to pass both Houses of the Legislature by a two-thirds majority in each. Once the Bill has passed both Houses, it goes in to the States. The second method prescribed is for a constitutional convention to be called by two-thirds of the Legislature of the States but this one has never been used. An amendment must be ratified, or approved, by three-quarters of States.

Of course there have been debates by American academics on the merits of the parliamentary system as an alternative to the presidential one but such debates have ended up endorsing the latter. The ever-expanding American nation has become more complex than it was when the constitution was promulgated in 1787, thirty-seven States having been added to the Union. Were the American people to opt for the parliamentary system of government today, the immediate impact would be the emergence of ethnic political parties and a weakened American nation. The reason America has been a two-party state for the greater part of its history is because of the unifying influence of the presidency.

Let me quickly remind readers here that America has meticulously kept a timetable of four-yearly presidential elections since 1789 when the first president was elected. If Barack Obama gets elected in November, most enthusiasts of fairness and racial equality hope he does, he will be sworn in as the forty-fourth and first African-American President of the United States in January 2009. This is the type of discipline and purposefulness one wishes for a Nigeria of one's dreams.

This writer's bias is for the presidential system of government and he makes no apology in asserting that Nigeria's borrowed presidential constitution has revealed greater potential for unity and stability than the erstwhile parliamentary system practised between 1960 and 1966. The presidential system is more or less a form of coalition that brings a heterogeneous group together. The president has the entire nation as his or her constituency, while the powers of government are shared responsibilities between the three arms of government. There is no basis for a "government of national unity" because, in an ideal situation, every political party that has an elected representative is inclusively in government.

Our experience of the parliamentary system is that of a nation partitioned into government and opposition along ethnic lines. The political parties were ethnic-based and political alliances were about which ethnic groups were prepared to work together. Every ethnic group had one derogatory name for the other and key politicians had no qualms about insulting the other group even on television. The outlook was never like it is with the nearly-homogeneous British people and each time we disagreed among ourselves we ended up calling for a government of national unity. The history of parliamentarism in Nigeria is a history of ethnic bickering and turbulence and one wonders why some are still nostalgic for it.

Of course it cannot be contradicted that the presidential system is a lot more expensive than the parliamentary one but its appropriateness for our society more than compensates for that. However, the cost of a chosen political arrangement must not be confused with the corruption and profligacy of political actors. The writer, Banji Adisa revealed in his patriotic article, "The high cost of governance", (*The Guardian*, 23 July 2008) that the Governor of Gombe State gave a parting cheque of N202 million (two hundred and two million naira) to his predecessor. This, in the eyes of decent people, is an act of financial profligacy for which the exuberant governor must be made to account. The level of financial recklessness in the Nigerian polity is endemic, a reflection of the quality of our political actors and the environment in which they operate. No state governor in the United States goes about dispensing public money as if it were his or her inheritance. The problem of accountability in our society invites urgent attention.

However, the position of this writer is that we should adapt the borrowed presidential system to the realities of our society. Many nations have succeeded in adapting either the presidential system or the parliamentary alternative; in fact, France and Switzerland have successfully married both. It makes sense for us to entrench the principle of leadership rotation in the constitution, not least because leadership has been the most contentious issue in our nation's history. Entrenching the principle of leadership rotation in the constitution could also tame our party system beyond current imagination.

Honestly, agitation for another constitutional conference – be it of ethnic nationalities or that of the intelligentsia – no longer excites. We have had too many conferences in the short history of our nation and maybe it is time we accepted that improving on what we already have is the way forward. The culture of election rigging undoubtedly deprives our "elected" men and women of legitimacy; otherwise, their right to improve on the constitution based on established procedures cannot be challenged. Of course the citizenry must remain active participants in both the legislative and governmental processes because their fortunes are inextricably tied to them.

*The Guardian, 06 August 2008*

# PART 2

# OBASANJO AND THE THIRD TERM STIGMA

## SYNOPSIS

*General Olusegun Obasanjo was the first elected president of an era Nigerians refer to as "The Third Republic". He had been the military leader between February 1976 and October 1979. His election as President came on the background of the annulled presidential election of 12 June 1993. That election could have concluded the transition programme from a military government led by General Ibrahim Babangida to a civilian government that would have been led by the presumed winner, Chief Moshood Abiola.*

*The annulment of an election adjudged to be "free and fair" was resented by right thinking Nigerians and the wave of public anger forced General Babangida to relinquish power.*

*Chief Abiola, a Yoruba philanthropist and business mogul from the south of Nigeria, sought to claim his mandate but was made to spend the rest of his life in detention by a succeeding military administration led by General Sani Abacha. Both Abacha and Abiola died in mysterious circumstances on 8 June 1998 and 7 July 1998 respectively.*

*The annulment of an election Nigerians simply refer to as "June 12" could not but have been resented by Nigerians in the south, not least because the leadership position had been dominated by their compatriots from the north. It was in the light of the ensuing crisis that another military government led by General Abdulsalami Abubakar "hurriedly" organised a transitional election, at which the presidency was conceded to the south. General Obasanjo, a Yoruba, contested the 1999 presidential election with another kinsman, Chief Olu Falae.*

*President Obasanjo's immediate preoccupation was to restore the image of Nigeria which had been badly damaged by the crisis emanating from the annulment, among other things. He did quite well in this regard, working hard as he did to secure "debt forgiveness" with the International Monetary Fund (IMF) and other*

46

*financial institutions. His experience as former ruler and soldier also helped to stabilise a nation troubled by Sharia politics and the nuisance of ethnic militia.*

*However, Obasanjo did not work hard enough to protect his own image which was badly rubbished by the suspicion that the constitutional changes he sought were of selfish interest, Specifically, it was believed he wanted to change the constitution so he could seek a third term in office. Nigeria's constitution allows a maximum of two terms of 4 years each.*

*Obasanjo's perceived ambition provoked a confrontation between him and his deputy, Alhaji Atiku Abubakar who also wanted to succeed his boss. Of course, Obasanjo was not the most honest manager of elections but the "third term agenda" is one stigma that has rubbished his modest achievements more than anything else.*

## Scoring The National Confab

One felt rather sorry for Justice Nikki Tobi, Chairman of the National Political Reform Conference, when he literally begged delegates to endorse some contentious positions as their present for his then impending 65th birthday. It was like asking a patient suffering from cancer to please accept treatment meant for malaria just to have on record that he or she had been attended to by a doctor. Contentious issues will always remain contentious until they are resolved by mutual compromise and agreements.

The National Political Reform Conference can be adjudged as successful, insofar as it provided the platform for the articulation of issues of importance to the various geo-political zones and ethnic nationalities. The delegates were well-respected members of their various constituencies and it is doubtful if representation via the electoral process could have produced a better outfit. The issues they highlighted can now be further appraised by those who by virtue of their constitutional positions have the powers to translate enlightened opinions into veritable legal documents for political practice.

The most disturbing of the contentious issues is that which has to do with resource control. The fact that oil is today the main source of our national survival cannot be over-exaggerated, so also is the fact that the oil wealth comes mainly from a section of the Nigerian community, the South-South geo-political zone. The oil producing region now insists on being paid 25% of revenue from oil, a percentage they would like to graduate to 50% over a 5-year period.

Their insistence on this position gives the writer much joy in certain respects. The first ground of support emanates from the belief that if the oil wealth had resided somewhere else, the issue of how much they wanted as payment would not have been "contentious". If the oil wealth had resided in the territory of one of the so-called majority ethnic groupings the so-called minority groups might have been made to feel grateful for the tiny crumbs that come in for them. The second ground of support is based on the sufferings which the oil producing areas have to endure due to environmental degradation. The effect of this on agriculture, fishing and even human health, cannot be over-stated. Finally, it is believed that increased revenue to the oil producing states may actually compel the non-producing ones to look inwards and develop other revenue earning sectors of the economy such as agriculture, industry and tourism. The fact that one region of the Nigerian society might actually be richer than the others is one inevitable aspect of federal relations we must learn to grapple with.

The tenure of the president, state governors and local government chairpersons is another contentious issue of interest. The tenure of the president, in particular, was further made contentious by the fact that the Obasanjo presidency was associated with the idea of a six-year single term for the president. This had been taken, in some quarters, as a devise by President Olusegun Obasanjo to extend his tenancy at Aso Rock. Had consistency been the forte of Obasanjo, such suspicion would not have enjoyed much attention because the six-year single term tenure was indeed the singular recommendation General Olusegun Obasanjo submitted to the Political Bureau instituted by the dictatorship of General Ibrahim Babadgida in 1986. President Obasanjo could have asserted that position in 2002 when the idea of single term presidency resurfaced with a vengeance. That would still not have stopped him from seeking re-election in 2003 because the constitution was on his side.

That the issue of the tenure of the president did take a North versus South divide is but one aspect of parochialism in our national politics. Insistence on two terms by some delegates from the North hinged on the argument that the current president who is from the South is in his second term of office and it would be unfair for one from the North not to enjoy the same status. For such a position to come from delegates whose region had dominated the leadership position for so long, it was one parochialism that was not in the best interests of national unity. This writer argued earlier that the endorsement of the principle of leadership rotation between the North and the South has effectively sealed the argument in favour of the single-term proposal. Otherwise it does not make much sense that a president is seeking re-election when challenge to his or her position can only come from the same zone. It is like one zone wanting to produce two presidents before another zone actually takes its turn.

It is not as if one is biased towards a section of the Nigerian society. Any nationalist of the mode of Colonel Abubakar Umar will agree that the concept of "one North, one people, one destiny" handed over by Lord Lugard and which became the article of faith for the ethnocentric Northern People's Congress (NPC), has never served the cause of Nigerian unity. The oneness of Nigeria is better served with the geo-political zones developing their individual characteristics. Fed up with the constant references to North and South and what the concepts connoted in Nigeria, the late Mr. David Williams, editor of the London-based West Africa magazine from 1945 to 1978, once suggested I advise the military to ban people talking of North and South. I told him that the only way to tame this divisive cleavage was by putting appropriate structures in place but will the beneficiaries of the cleavage system allow such structures to work?

Now on the issue of whether or not to ban former rulers from seeking the coveted office of president, there was this friend of mine, an enthusiastic supporter of General Ibrahim Babangida, who strongly believed that his idol would be the next president of Nigeria. He sought my opinion on what should be the title of his proposed book celebrating the second coming of Babangida. I did not pause to think and we both laughed when I told him the title of his proposed book should be "O, ye fools, I am back".

The culture of banning belongs to military authoritarianism; however reflecting on what the power of stolen money can do in a corrupt electoral system, the proposed ban would appear not to be out of place. The well-informed Americans know that a Richard Nixon has no moral right to even dream of wanting to become their president for a second time, but one cannot be too sure of what a Nigerian population humiliated and humbled by poverty will do when a worse than Richard Nixon "politician" appears at the corridors, in the full regalia of a Father Christmas, dishing out bundles of crisp naira notes!

*This Day, 24 July 2005*

# Possible Fall outs From Third Term Debate

One irony of the third term issue is that General Olusegun Obasanjo who vacated office voluntarily as a military ruler in 1979 and was accorded great respect by the international community for his "uncommon African feat" is today at the centre of a sit-tight controversy. His "intention" to remain in office beyond the limit of two terms permitted by the 1999 Constitution may or may not be informed by patriotic reasons but the choice we have made in Nigeria is that of a constitutional democracy powered by a periodic change of leadership and ideas. The monotonous and nauseating argument that Obasanjo has no credible alternative can therefore only impress the apologist of political dictators and sit-tight rulers.

If political greatness is measured by the length of time a political actor spent in office, Africa's past and present leaders would be in the upper league and those of the advanced democratic nations of the world in the lower one. Political greatness is about responding positively and decisively to the most pressing challenge of one's generation. Even when Obasanjo is a successful Nigerian leader by all relative and comparative accounts, it is doubtful if he would achieve the greatness he seeks by destroying what could have amounted to a great legacy in the eyes of history. The culture of periodic democratic leadership change, if spear- headed by the first political leader that Obasanjo is in our new Nigerian Republic is, in itself, a platform for greatness and political immortality.

The political arrangement mimicked by Nigeria is America's, so it is not out of place to say something about the nation's political leadership. George Washington, America's first President, is not remembered as an economic miracle worker; the respect accorded to his great name emanated from the manner in which he established the principles of democracy and constitutional government in the American nation. When Richard Nixon, America's 36th President, got himself enmeshed in the Watergate scandal Americans said he violated the legacy of George Washington. John F. Kennedy did not even complete a four-year tenure but his name is right there among those of great presidents because of what he accomplished within a very short period of time.

A great political leader provides the yardstick or standard by which others are judged. Because he was a small man with oversized boots, Mobutu Zeze-Zeko could not provide Zaireans with a positive legacy in spite of more than thirty years of political leadership. Robert Mugabe started very well, as the free world acclaimed him for leading his people to freedom and independence from the trenches. He has since become a pariah in civilized circles because he had long outlived his usefulness. Obasanjo may have helped in resolving our debt burden but is it not a sad pointer that those who made "debt forgiveness" possible are today viewing him with some contempt because of the third term confusion?

The third term agenda can only lead to a major crisis, not least because of the belligerent manner with which it is being pursued. If third term is "forced" unto the constitution the proponents will translate it into an accomplished task in 2007, even if it requires the rigging of elections. The crisis warning the proponents may arrogantly want to ignore will come to the fore when the outcome of the presidential election is violently contested. The third term controversy may not have polarized society along ethnic or religious sympathies, not least because the presidency has succeeded in tying its own greed with those of state governors so it could be predicted that a crisis situation could be a free-for-all street fighting.

It can no longer be said that President Obasanjo's quest for a third term in office is "alleged", because it is now real. The president himself has said that a further term in office would enable him to anchor his programmes – an ambition that has been pursued both ruthlessly and crudely by the leadership of his party, the People's Democratic Party (PDP).

"Obasanjoism" is a strange element in modern, democratic philosophy. The tactics President Obasanjo employs tend to play on the intelligence of Nigerians. The military tactics of secrecy and keeping the opposition guessing may be admirable in a war situation but it is one tactic that could be deemed odd in some democratic cultures and circumstances. Even when Obasanjo has already made up his mind on what he would do he tells Nigerians he is still consulting God. The larger public may or may not endorse it, a major presidential address formally seeking the understanding and support of Nigerians would have been the intelligent and polite approach if an elongated tenure was indeed in our national interest. There may be a time in the life of a nation – a state-of-war for instance – when an exception could be granted to the rule.

The two terms limit was of a conventional practice in America until 1951 when it was formally entrenched in the Constitution. The Great Depression of the 1930s and America's involvement in the Second World War were factors which combined in favour of Delano Roosevelt winning three elections. Roosevelt's economic reforms were monumental, provoking what is until today acknowledged as the greatest political realignment in American history – the massive shift of Black American voters from Abraham Lincoln's Republican Party of Emancipation to the reformist Democratic Party.

Take the unsubstantiated allegations of bribery out of the scene, one would say that the ongoing debate on the third term agenda is healthy for the future of democracy in Nigeria. Of course motives compete and contrast in a debate of this nature, one nevertheless believes that the most important outcome, especially if third term is defeated, would be the establishment of the primacy of constitutional principles in our democracy. The impact would not only reflect on the tenure of the president but generally on the critical provisions of the Nigerian Constitution. If, for instance, the principle of leadership rotation is entrenched in the Constitution no group can unilaterally change it for selfish reasons.

The one other good thing one sees about this debate is that "for and against" cuts across ethnic and religious boundaries. The Yoruba has not supported third term overwhelmingly on the grounds that the incumbent President is a member of their group. Prominent Yoruba activists like Chief Gani Fawehinmi and Professor Wole Soyinka have been at the forefront of anti third term campaigns. Their respect for constitutionality and lack of ambition for ethnic hold on political power is commendable. Embracing the principles of fairness and constitutionality will do the unity of Nigeria a world of good if at all times such principles know no ethnic or religious discriminations.

*The Gamji, 23 May 2006*

# Fanaticism in a fragile state

Anyone electing to write the story of the Olusegun Obasanjo presidency should not allow misgivings over the ludicrous third term ambition or the embarrassing feud between President and Vice President to obscure the administration's success or otherwise in conflict management. Hurricane, *Sharia* and ethnic militia politics once presented our nation with such a dilemma that it would be unwise to quickly forget the dangers they posed.

This is a personal opinion, and who says one is not entitled to it, that President Obasanjo approached the *Sharia* issue with great calm and got a justified result? The popular opinion in the south of Nigeria was that the spread of *Sharia* in the manner it did was intended to undermine the legitimacy of the Obasanjo administration. Had Obasanjo not been tactful or patient he probably would have played into the hands of the *Sharia* proponents. If *Sharia* was not politically motivated, the practicing states should by now be reaping the rewards of an environment that is free from corruption and other social ills.

As for Nigeria's ethnic militias, their origin can be traced to the misrule of General Sani Abacha and the confusion it brought. However, it was one nuisance the Obasanjo administration had to contend with. It was as if the Nigerian state was on its way to collapse, with every major component of the federation represented by a quasi-military outfit of some sort. Obasanjo decisively denied the ethnic militias the legitimacy they forcefully and violently sought but he may only have succeeded in driving them underground.

The point one is trying to make here is that the Nigerian state has not yet come to stay. Nigerian nationalists cannot go to their final sleep today convinced they would reincarnate the Nigeria of their dreams. Share population and economic resources make Nigeria a potential major player in global politics. Envious they may be, other Africans see Nigeria as a beacon of hope for the African continent and the black race and its citizens as privileged. Nollywood has become

Hollywood for Africans who scramble in Europe and America for Nigerian films. But will the fanatics amongst us allow the Nigerian dream to be fulfilled?

This article responds to a recent report in the Nigerian Tribune that fanatics were planning attacks on churches and co-citizens of Nigeria in the aftermath of the execution of the Iraqi dictator Saddam Hussein. How has Nigeria come to the equation in an affair in which no Nigerian was remotely involved? How many Nigerians fought on the side of the American and British troops who succeeded in ending the tyranny of Saddam Hussein, albeit for their own selfish interests? Did the Nigerian government ever make a stand in the second Iraq conflict, either before or after the execution of Saddam Hussein?

A report of this nature would have been dismissed out of hand had an event in far away Denmark not led to killings and wanton destruction of property in Nigeria. About a year ago some misguided and ignorant cartoonists depicted the Holy Prophet Mohammed rather derogatively. Muslims and right thinking Christians were equally infuriated. There were understandable protests in major cities of the world but in Nigeria we chose to go the extra mile of taking revenge on our own people. The reprisals which followed in another section of our society should be a warning to all of us that a free-for-all ethnic fighting is not an impossible scenario in Nigeria.

To keep Nigeria one may have once been a compulsory military task but it is a task that must now find its destination in our homes, educational institutions, and religious places of worship. Our soldiers have become fat and worldly so that no one is ready for the trenches! We must continue to educate ourselves about the ethics of good neighbourliness and what a peaceful and prosperous Nigerian nation means for all of us and our children's children.

The diversity of the Nigerian nation should be a source of strength and not weakness. The major nations of the world are becoming increasingly diverse and multi-racial by the day, as the Nigerian population is also becoming noticeable outside the Nigerian borders.

Nigerians in diaspora have a moral duty to continue to promote the unity and continued existence of Nigeria as one nation, not least because they themselves have become component units of other nations.

The much discussed American intelligence report did not say categorically that Nigeria will become a failed state. What the report suggested was that the potentials for disintegration are quite evident. Even the most patriotic amongst us should not be blind to the fact that ours is a fragile nation. The brutal truth is that there are Nigerians who, for their own reasons, do not believe in the concept of "One Nigeria" and would scream with joy if the "unthinkable" were to happen. They are Nigerians who must be persuaded to the common cause by a new Nigerian nation that is fair to its citizens and the collective aspirations of the groups they represent.

Superpowers (Britain, the Soviet Union and the USA) were historic and unlikely allies in the Nigerian Civil War of 1967-70. Nigeria might not be one nation today if these superpowers had not lent their support to the mission of the Yakubu Gowon-led Federal Government. Should we again put our nation in a situation whereby external intervention becomes inevitable, their position on the Nigerian question could be a u-turn. They have supervised the collapse and partitioning of many fragile nations in recent years and anyone who thinks America is not a lot more comfortable with the Gambias and Lesothos of this world than a Nigerian nation posturing as a superpower in the making, wanting to be a member of the exclusive security council, requires a few lessons in international politics to appreciate the message of this article.

I was in America in the early 1980s when Samuel Doe of Liberia visited Ronald Reagan. He had come to beg for money. Reagan was going to introduce him but it appeared he had forgotten his name. He chuckled and said, "meet our friend, Chairman Moe". How the American Presidents love those humble leaders of tiny and harmless countries!

*The Guardian 15 January 2007*

# Obasanjo and History

THE final chapter of President Olusegun Obasanjo's political history as national leader of the Federal Republic of Nigeria is fast approaching its conclusion. Obasanjo's physical presence may remain with us for many more years to come but that would be a matter of less interest than it currently is. How are we going to remember him and what could be his legacy? I ask these questions because what people remember a contemporary leader for may not necessarily constitute a legacy in the eyes of history. What then is a legacy?

The Oxford Dictionary of English defines legacy as "something left or handed down by a predecessor (the legacy of centuries of neglect)". As a matter of fact, most past political leaders merely occupied space and did not leave permanent footprints in the sands of time. A legacy, positive or negative, is an event whose consequences endure in history. For instance, the continuing transformation of the Yoruba into a community of assertive and highly educated people is the legacy of the legendary Obafemi Awolowo's policy of universal free primary education implemented in the 1950's, If President Obasanjo is destined to be a political leader with an enduring legacy, it could be from one of the many things he did while in office.

One irony of President Olusegun Obasanjo is that he will be leaving behind him an image of the Nigerian nation almost as he met it in 1999, an image of contempt in the eyes of the world. President Obasanjo's immediate preoccupation upon coming to power was to redeem an image which General Sani Abacha would appear to have left battered beyond repair. Obasanjo did this with utmost commitment, as his became a ubiquitous face in every capital of the world, trying to sell Nigeria to those who had assumed it was a better forgotten place. His persistence would appear to have paid off but the image of Nigeria as a crude African nation has again re-emerged in the same capitals, not least because of rigged elections whose scale and methodology defy civilized imaginations. Those touting Obasanjo as a possible Nobel Prize winner for his role in conflict management in the African continent would now be rushing to withdraw their signatures!

The truth is that contemporary Nigerians, especially those less sympathetic to Obasanjo and his political party, will continue to emphasise the 2007 elections and the bickering between him and his deputy, Vice President Atiku Abubakar, as the key moments of his presidency. Dr Tajudeen Abdul-Raheem in a recent article, described President Olusegun Obasanjo as a "Field Marshal in the art of manufacturing enemies". Obasanjo's combatant approach to politics could not but have earned him a few enemies. He is one politician who pays scant regard to image making; there are quite a few things he did which could have got the entire nation singing behind him if he had had a more polished way of selling himself in the political market. The fight against corruption should be a national fight which, on its own, could have constituted an enduring legacy for a great political leader. The few scapegoats of our war against corruption ended up getting undeserved sympathy because it was one war many believed or assumed Obasanjo had directed against real and perceived enemies or those he had disagreed with.

However, assuming the war against corruption continues to feature in the agenda of future governments and corruption itself becomes an unattractive venture among future generations of Nigerians, the name of Olusegun Obasanjo will be written in gold. He was right to want to support a political leader who he believed would continue with his reform programme. What he was not right to do was to insist on it as the national choice via the instrumentality of election rigging.

General Obasanjo is an apostle of a one-party state, an author of a book in that subject. The massive rigging he and Maurice Iwu of the "Independent" National Electoral Commission (INEC) orchestrated was geared towards achieving Obasanjo's dream of a one-party Nigeria. He again gave this away in a recent speech, the relevant part of which I quote here: "... I believe that if the National Assembly is an arm of government, National Assembly should not be an opposition to the Executive arm of government. They should work together particularly when they are now from the same party" (The Guardian, 8 May 1997).

Our president's statement betrays a lack of understanding for the workings of the presidential system of government which he has superintended for eight good years. Or, he is still angry that his "third term" agenda did not sail through! The freedom of elected politicians to vote according to their individual consciences, the majority opinion in the constituencies they represent, and indeed their own future political aspirations, have combined to provide the lubricant that keeps the engine of the principle of Separations of Powers working. The Nigerian politicians who seek to wrestle power form the People's Democratic Party (PDP) must now begin to work towards producing an alternative or rival political party for future governance. I say "alternative" or "rival" political party because parties of presidential politics are not "opposition" parties in the context of adversarial politics; the parties are expected to be able to work together.

Of course President Olusegun Obasanjo will be remembered for his part in getting Nigeria out of debt but this would only be for as long as the country is not back to the bad old ways. His critics are however not happy that Obasanjo boasts more of what money he has saved in the bank than what he has been able to do for the nation in terms of jobs, and social and infrastructural developments. Obasanjo's era also heralded a new culture of widespread use of the telephone but to over emphasise this would be like wanting to attribute the use of motor vehicles to a particular government in Nigeria. Nigeria did not invent the telephone so there should be little noise about it. There are things which contemporary Nigerians should be taking for granted which, sadly, still remain in their dreams – things like the uninterrupted supply of electricity and free-flowing drinkable water. Obasanjo's success rating, as is the case with any other political leader, will vary from one individual to the other. However, what constitutes his legacy, if any, is a matter for the undiscriminating eyes of history to reveal.

*The Guardian, 23 May 2007*

# PART 3

# YAR'ADUA AND EXAGGERATED REFORMS

## SYNOPSIS

*In the aftermath of General Olusegun Obasanjo's failed third term agenda, one seeming determination of his was not to be succeeded by his deputy, Alhaji Atiku Abubakar. Obasanjo sought a successor of selfish choice in Umaru Musa Yar'Adua who was the younger brother of his bosom friend and erstwhile "second-in-command" while military ruler, the late Major-General Shehu Musa Yar'Adua. The health condition of Umaru Yar'Adua was worrying, prompting political commentators of northern origin to insinuate that the reason Obasanjo wanted Yar'Adua to be president was because he knew he would not last in office and the presidency would shift to the south sooner than expected. Yar'Adua did die in office and the presidency fell to his erstwhile deputy, Goodluck Jonathan; however, the opinion of the author of this book is that Obasanjo chose Umaru Musa Yar'Adua to be president because of the warm relationship he enjoyed with his senior brother who died in Sani Abacha's detention.*

*Be that as it may, the 2007 election that brought Yar'Adua into office was hardly free and fair. Obasanjo tagged the 2007 presidential election "Operation do-or-die". Yar'Adua himself was honest that the election was flawed, promising to institute reforms. He, indeed, established a committee for reforms under the leadership of retired Justice Muhammadu Uwais but the committee's main recommendations have yet to be implemented.*

*One of President Yar'Adua's main achievements was in stemming the tide of revolt in the oil producing region of the Nigerian federation, the Niger Delta. Readers wanting to know more about this and the politics of his incapacity and eventual death, are invited to read the interesting book by his adviser on Media Affairs, Olusegun Adeniyi, Power, Politics and Death – A front row account of Nigeria under the late President Yar'Adua (Prestige 2011).*

# Yar'adua`s legitimacy problem

Three factors conspire to pose initial problems for President Umaru Yar'Adua. The fact that he was relatively unknown should be the least and most temporary of such problems. As our nation progresses in democracy, candidates not quite known to the national constituency (dark horses) will continue to emerge as presidential contestants and possibly presidents. That has been the case even in the United States of America where most presidents have been recruited from the ranks of governors, senators and vice-presidents. Jimmy Carter was not a prominent national figure until becoming president in 1976 and the same can be said of the current president – always in the shadow of his father, former President George W. Bush (Snr) – when he came to the national scene in 2000. Jimmy Carter was governor of Georgia, while George Bush presided over the state of Texas. Acknowledged as a successful governor of Katsina state, Umaru Musa Yar'Adua would appear to have acquired the experience he needed to perform at the level he now finds himself. Just like Carter and Bush, he should grow in stature and confidence with time.President Yar'Adua's second problem can be described as the "Obasanjo factor". Unlike former President Shehu Shagari whose sole ambition was to be senator until persuaded to run for the presidency, there is nothing to suggest Yar'Adua was not quite enthusiastic about the prospect of being President of the Federal Republic of Nigeria. However, the fact that former President Olusegun Obasanjo more or less single-handedly imposed him on the People's Democratic Party (PDP) and consequently on our nation, is an open secret to all of us. In this regard, many have assumed that the Yar'Adua presidency could be an extension of the Obasanjo presidency by proxy – an assumption which Mr Yar'Adua must dismiss at the earliest possible opportunity. General Obasanjo can be supportive of the Yar'Adua presidency; however, should he start to flaunt his influence with the arrogance of a godfather, Yar'Adua should be cutting him down to size to the delight of all of us.

The third and perhaps most critical problem confronting Alhaji Yar'Adua is how to legitimise a presidency that has been badly tainted by flawed electoral outcome – a legitimacy problem that would still be there even if the president is vindicated by the election tribunal and the courts. It would seem, therefore, that the best thing President Yar'Adua can do in the present circumstances is to plot a strategy of how he could gradually worm his way into the hearts of Nigerians via the manner in which he approaches the governance of state and society. This point was elaborately made by Dr Reuben Abati in his article, "Yar'Adua: The Twist in the Tale", (The Guardian, June 3, 2007) in which he advised President Yar'Adua, among other things, to run an inclusive government rather than the winner-takes-all one. What this writer seeks to emphasise here is the need for President Yar'Adua to embark on reforming the electoral process even in the first year of his administration.

The 2007 elections are a national shame and disgrace, a fact which President Yar'Adua himself tacitly acknowledged in his inaugural speech. His promise to work towards bringing the Nigerian electoral process in line with civilized practices is welcome and soothing. The position this writer has expressed on the current state of our nation is that of continuously reforming our democratic institutions and processes regardless. Dr G A Akinola of the University of Ibadan's Department of History made a valid point (The Guardian, May 20, 2007) that the current National Assembly, dominated by PDP members as it is, could be more interested in entrenching their group interest than instituting genuine reforms. His is one informed assertion or scepticism which President Yar'Adua must seek to disprove.

If the electoral process is to be reformed, it may be one exercise which would constitute a part of the comprehensive review of the 1999 Constitution itself. In the current atmosphere of national distrust President Yar'Adua would be doing himself a world of good by conveying a constitutional conference, different from the Obasanjo "third term" one that would look into critical issues in our society. Such a conference would have knowledgeable Nigerians as its members. Of course members of the legislature are the elected law-makers in our society but the fact of a manufactured one-party dominance could rubbish the outcome of a constitutional review if left to them alone. Sceptics might dismiss a new Constitution as a "PDP manifesto".

In reviewing the electoral process in particular, emphasis must be on how to constitute an electoral commission whose independence and impartiality are beyond doubt. The problematic voters' register is a permanent record that is merely updated. The current Nigerian government should establish registries in every local government headquarters and pass a law which mandates every birth and death in our society to be registered. The National Identity scheme introduced by the Obasanjo administration should become a permanent feature of our culture.

We must aim to decongest future elections and one mechanism which could help in achieving this is to stagger them. We could borrow from the American practice, without having to copy it. The American President serves a term of four years; senators six years; members of the House of Representatives two years. There may be a need for us to rethink new terms of office for elected politicians.

The thinking of the American constitutionalists was that a member of the House of Representatives would be an effective delegate of his or her local constituency if subjected to frequent elections, whereas the more mature senator was acknowledged as representing state and national interests rather than parochial local interests.

We must be "scientific" in whatever provisions or recommendations we make in a reviewed constitution. Now that we are coming to appreciate and acknowledge the relevance and suitability of rotational presidency in our society, one could be arguing for a single term presidency of six or seven years tenure in the near future. If we agree to write "rotation" in the constitution, and who says we should not, re-electing a future president may not make sense. The principle of rotation will make a salutary impact on the development of the Nigerian party system.

President Umaru Yar'Adua must know that the greatest honour history can confer on any individual is the rare privilege of being leader of one's own nation. Sadly, small men in over sized shoes do not appreciate the full import of living forever in history for they only assume leadership to be an opportunity to enrich themselves and their cronies. The fact that no one has been saying that Yar'Adua was a corrupt governor of Katsina state suggests our nation may be in healthy hands after all.

*The Guardian, 13 June 2007*

# Beyond Yar'Adua's tainted victory

Only Professor Maurice Iwu, Chairman of the 'Independent' National Electoral Commission (INEC) and beneficiaries of the recently concluded national elections, will call for a celebration of the outcome. The elections have been rightly described as a charade, a monumental failure by any yardstick of honesty. President Olusegun Obasanjo may have done irretrievable damage to his own legacy, not least because of his 'do or die' approach to the nation's electoral contest.

Maurice Iwu proudly told Nigerians they had successfully overcome the jinx of failed elections. If he were to be honest with himself, he should have realised that the cause of our historical jinx has been the culture of electoral fraud, which his own commission has further perpetuated. Declared winner and therefore president-elect, one feels rather sorry for Governor Umar Yar'Adua because the victory he might have achieved regardless is tainted in the eyes of the world.

In terms of organisation and endowment with the resources of state power, the People's Democratic Party (PDP) was the one to beat. Pitched against opposition parties most of which were mere vehicles for the expression of exaggerated ambitions, Mr Yar-Adua could probably still have won a respectable and dignified victory if elections were free and fair. Regarded as a man of integrity, one not too frightened to declare his assets, he would now need all the skills he could possibly muster to legitimize a position his rivals may be unwilling to concede to him.

If the spirit of reconciliation eventually prevails and Alhaji Yar-Adua becomes president on May 29, his immediate task would be to establish his authority on his party and the Nigerian State. Many believe, righty or wrongly, that a Yar-Adua presidency is an extension of an Obasanjo presidency by proxy, an assumption he must quickly dispel. The president is 'first without equal', the entire nation being his constituency. The positions he takes on national issues must be informed by our collective interests and not exclusively those of the political party to which he belongs. He would need to renounce whatever 'oath of allegiance' to which he might have sworn, because the so-called oath of allegiance is informed by fear and the selfish interests of its priests. The principle of Separation of Powers, which is the engine of our borrowed system, abhors one arm of government colluding with another. In a system that does not recognise institutionalised opposition, one arm of government checks and balances the other(s). The fact of a one-party dominance does not obscure the importance and sacredness of this principle or doctrine.

The way forward for the Nigerian nation is for politicians to reconcile their selfish interest with our collective interests. I describe most of Nigeria's political parties as 'mere vehicles for the expression of exaggerated ambitions' because there is hardly anything to suggest one of the fifty-odd parties is different from the other. The very essence of their existence is because certain individuals wanted to be president. The so-called political parties were not divided on issues and all that their leaders kept promising us was the supply of water and electricity- the same promises the politicians of pre-independence Nigeria had made fifty years ago.

Most of Nigeria's politicians believed in nothing other than their individual selfish ambitions. Not being good team players, the politicians were too quick to switch political affiliation and support once their immediate aspirations were not met. The bitter lesson they must now learn is that mushroom political parties have little place in presidential politics. Had the opposition parties consolidated themselves into a formidable rival party, the PDP and INEC might not have succeeded in perpetrating election rigging on the scale to which they did. The choice most voters were confronted with would also have been better clarified. This, however, is not saying that there can be a circumstance under which the most minute spectre of rigging is justified.

One good thing emerging from the crucible of our national mess is the seeming consensus that military intervention in politics is no longer an option. With continuity of the democratic order, the contradiction of state and society can be resolved given time. Military intervention makes us a perpetual 'begin again' people each time the soldiers decide we could have an election. Democracy itself is a culture that is not just about the periodic exercise of electoral mandate but the acceptance of the fact that we all owe equal loyalty to the political order. The nations whose democracies we now envy fought continuously through a series of reforms to be where they are today. There was once a time when the black American was not allowed to vote because his or her grandfather did not vote! How could the grandfather who was a slave, counted as a fraction of a human being for the purpose of taxation and representation, have voted?

The only way forward is one that leads to the future. Eight years of democracy have not been a total failure. The press has prospered and revelled in the type of freedom military rulers were too eager to deny. The judicial arm of government, which is the last hope of the ordinary Nigerian, has been asserting its independence with enviable determination. There have been landmark decisions of nightmarish consequences for Obasanjo and his close associates, the type of decisions that generals Ibrahim Babangida and Sami Abacha would once have ignored with arrogance. The same judiciary must now look into cases of electoral malpractice and fearlessly sort things out.

There have been cases of candidates for election who did not find their names on the ballot papers; their cases call for a rerun of elections, or adequate payment of compensation for their time and electoral expenses where a rerun of elections may not make sense. The future of democracy rests with Nigerians and an electoral umpire whose independence and impartiality are beyond doubt. Of course the next pilot of the Nigerian state could be a president who genuinely believes in democracy and its ideals, unlike one whose natural inclination and professional orientation revolt against democratic norms.

There may have been a lot of anger over the outcome of elections in 2007; however, unlike in previous failed transition elections, our anger has not translated into inter-ethnic abuses or confrontations. No one has accused INEC of favouritism towards one geo-political group or the other. This development I attribute to the fact that the major presidential contestants were from the same region- a further argument for the appropriateness of a system of leadership rotation in our polity.

*The Guardian 03 May 2007*

## Constitution: Issues of priority

The assumption here is that a comprehensive review of the Constitution may be difficult to achieve given the limited time at our disposal. Our law-makers dissipated so much time and energy bickering over privileges and matters of ego that there is hardly sufficient time left in the life of the current assembly to do an honest job. However, it is important that we improve on what we already have and selective amendment of existing provisions of the Constitution may be the realistic option in the present circumstances.

The case for selective amendment is all the more attractive if our problem is not with the skeletal framework on which the Constitution itself is built. For instance, one assumes that majority opinion still favours federalism and presidentialism. If, however, the contrary is the case then our peoples will be justified in demanding a total overhaul of the Constitution.

Every aspect of the Constitution is important but there are some issues with greater implications for the stability of our nation than others. The history of our nation may suggest that such issues are accorded priority. One is tempted to identify the ongoing Niger Delta controversy, the presidency and future elections as issues of priority. One would therefore attempt to briefly discuss each of these issues, not necessarily in their order of importance.

One suspects our law-makers may now actually want to review or amend the Constitution! It was reported recently that some of our senators were quite excited by the idea of independent candidacy. In fact the recommendation by the Uwais-led Electoral Reform Committee may have been the carrot dangled before our politicians. What independent candidacy means to our elected politicians is that those of them who may not be presented by their political parties for re-election in 2011 could still put their names forward as independent candidates. When it comes to matters of selfish interest, who says politicians are not the smartest?

The idea of independent candidacy may be attractive but it is not the most important of the recommendations made by the Electoral Reform Committee. With fifty political parties registered for elections, we are never short of platforms for desperate politicians to contest in elections. The honest truth is that our electoral system is lousy and our elected leaders are dodgy. The same society where a mere 65 year old professor is considered to be no longer suitable to continue in the university system had no qualms about elevating a fragile 75 year old granny to supervise an election in a most volatile state of the Nigerian Federation! What our law-makers should be warming up to, if there is any honesty in them, is how to make our electoral institution truly independent and also how to put in place a timeframe for the resolution of electoral disputes before elected men and women are sworn into office.

The presidency is another issue, but let something first be said about the legislative arm of government. The legislature is the engine of our democracy, an arena where men and women of quality might continue to make their presence felt. The tenure of the members is unlimited and that is how it should be for the honest pugilist of the cause of his or her own constituency. From John F. Kennedy to Barack Obama, the United States, for instance, has had ten different presidents in as much time as Edward Kennedy has been senator. Three of those presidents (Ronald Reagan, Bill Clinton and George W. Bush) actually completed two terms in office.

The position of president, however, is powerful and prestigious and that explains why the institution of leadership is identified as one that has the capacity to unite or tear apart our fragile nation. The leadership issue should be settled in the life of the current assembly and the suggestion here is that rotating the presidency along defined ethno-sectional constituencies will bring peace. A new term of office for the president – a single term for that matter – cannot and must not be construed as an attempt to elongate the tenure of the incumbent president. If President Musa Yar' Adua successfully seeks re-election in 2011, the new term of office for president will have a future effect from 2015.

It must be emphasised that designing a unique political arrangement does not make our nation any less democratic than others. What makes a nation democratic or not is the extent to which it respects agreed rules and procedures. The so-called advanced democratic nations of the world have varied political arrangements – the presidential/congressional system in America, the Westminster parliamentary system in the United Kingdom, the presidential/parliamentarianism in France and the collective presidency in Switzerland. Why must Nigeria be the copycat nation?

However, the most urgent task before us is how to bring sanity to the Niger Delta controversy. The Niger Delta imbroglio is about our collective economic existence and it is also about economic justice for those whose lands produce the national wealth. The answer to the crisis may not be in our attempt to bully agitators into submission; rather, it demands an informed dialogue leading to compromise.

The long term solution to the Niger Delta crisis may be in reviving other sectors of the economy which, sadly, became neglected on the arrival of easy oil money. The agricultural sector needs to be revived – cocoa in the south west, oil palm in the south east and groundnut in particular in the north. The various schools of agriculture and farm institutes also need to be revived or improved to absorb a teaming population of unemployed men and women whose talents can be put to productive use.

The years of oil wealth have merely produced more kleptocrats. Our governments lack the talent to create wealth and because the majority of our peoples are poor, their contributions to the national wealth are almost nil. How can society develop, and its peoples enjoy the facilities of modern civilisation, when they do not pay taxes or bills?

*The Nigeria Tribune 17 August 2009*

# A culture of lousy reforms

ONE would have assumed that if one recommendation of the Electoral Reform Committee was going to be accepted without much deliberation, it would be the one suggesting a period of six months for the resolution of electoral disputes before elected men and women are sworn into office. That the Federal Executive Council did not consider this recommendation to be sufficiently important speaks volumes about the collective sense of judgment of its members. For more than 17 months, the legitimacy of incumbent President Umaru Musa Yar'Adua was disputed in the courts of law; one would have thought that, on the basis of personal experience, he would be the one arguing vigorously in support of this recommendation.

Honestly, were this writer to be a member of the Electoral Reform Committee he would have argued for a shorter period of three months. He would have anchored his argument on the need to reduce the number of elections we are confronted with by staggering them into different years. Resolving election disputes should be a matter of priority in an election year and there should be no need for it to drag on for too long.

Look for instance at how swiftly the disputed election in the State of Florida was resolved when Al Gore contested the American presidency with George W. Bush in the year 2000 and look also at the fact that even when Barack Obama was elected President on November 4, 2008 he did not assume that position until January 20, 2009.

The American constitutionalists, intelligent human beings that they were, made provision for a reasonable space of time between the conclusion of presidential election and inauguration of a new president into office.

Hopefully, when the National Assembly deliberate on the White Paper report, they will permit their judgement to be informed by experience, common sense and what is good for the Nigerian nation. They ought to know that someone who did not win an election should not, under any circumstances, be allowed to assume the position of President of the Federal Republic of Nigeria or governor of any state in the federation - even for just one day. The oath of office is sacred; it should not be administered when we are in doubt. Remember that Barack Obama swore to the oath of office twice, albeit because of a minor mistake in the first instance and that should inform us that some societies take it seriously.

Also to be guided by experience and commonsense is our choice of who is chairperson of the Independent National Electoral Commission. The adjective 'independent' would have been corrupted if the President who happened to be a member of a political party is the one appointing that chairperson. The Electoral Reform Committee recommended that the power of appointing the chairperson of the Commission be vested in the National Judicial Council but the Federal Executive Council rejected their recommendation on the ground that the principle of Separation of Powers would be compromised if such a power were conferred on the body.

However, Dr. Reuben Abati in a well-researched and well-argued article, "Electoral Reform and the Federal Executive Council", (The Guardian, March 13, 2009) highlighted diverse practices in a few African nations which, in itself, is to suggest that we may not have exhausted all available options on this rather controversial and highly sensitive issue. The argument for ensuring that the National Electoral Commission is truly independent is as compelling as that of not dragging the judicial arm of government into the messy waters of politics.

Not so controversial is the idea of independent candidacy which has been understandably hailed by Nigerians. In a society where everyone wants to be President or Governor, how will such a provision not go down so well? Of course this writer endorses the idea of independent candidacy but is not too sure if it will enhance the quality of our democratic practices. It is a matter of wait and see.

In the run-up to the 2007 elections, about 50 political parties were registered and about 25 candidates contested the presidency. The number of contestants could easily have flooded the electoral space if independent candidacy were then part of our democratic culture. A lot of work will have to be done on this provision if it becomes law, to ensure that it is not open to abuse. The independent candidate, in the American presidential election parlance, is referred to as 'third party'. He or she knows that the presidency is not there to be won by an independent candidate, but is in the race because an issue he or she identifies with may have been ignored by the main political parties. If such an issue has implications for electoral outcome, a major political party may expediently absorb it. In short, Americans do not frivolously exploit the independent candidacy opportunity, not least because of enormous financial implications.

There was this moaning about proportional representation not being injected into the electoral system. Honestly, if this idea was presented to the Federal Executive Council and they rejected it, it is a job well done. Those who propose ideas should learn to do so in the context of our political arrangement and this is not to say that they are not entitled to advocate a change. Our representative democracy is personality-based, not party-based.

The senator, for instance, represents a senatorial district. You do not just assign senatorial seats to a political party simply because it has won a certain percentage of votes. The Americans do not have proportional representation because it is inappropriate to their political arrangement and the British do not want it because it would merely proliferate the political space with mushroom political parties - some kind of invitation to political instability.

Reform is desirable, especially in a society where such a reform can lead to positive changes. Reform is not just about institutional framework or provisions but significantly about the human factor. The thieves we rightly identified in our war against corruption and made so much noise about, are today dictating political and economic terms in their various states. In fact, they are fighting back and Mr. Nuhu Ribadu can testify to this. So much for a culture of lousy reforms.

*The Guardian, 19 March 2009*

# PART 4

# JONATHAN AND THE ZONING CONTROVERSY

## SYNOPSIS

*The politics of Nigeria has little or no ideological content; what divides Nigerians are their ethnicity and religion. Following the death of President Umaru Musa Yar'Adua on 5 May 2010, Goodluck Jonathan became president of the federation by virtue of the provisions of the constitution. He had been acting in that capacity once the incapacity of Yar'Adua was no longer deniable.*

*However, the 2011 election was also approaching and the question of who would be the flag-bearer of the ruling Peoples Democratic Party (PDP) became a highly contentious issue. The PDP operated a "zoning and rotation" principle of alternating the presidency between the North and South. General Olusegun Obasanjo, a member of the PDP had been president for two terms in office and had Yar'Adua been alive and healthy, he probably would have completed the northern "slot". President Goodluck Jonathan understood his precarious situation, suggesting that running again as a vice presidential candidate with a northern presidential candidate would not be beyond his contemplation. Jonathan must have been prevailed upon to seek election by his more hardened supporters as they embarked on an opportunistic denial of an agreement Jonathan himself was said to have been party to. General Olusegun Obasanjo, a supporter of Jonathan, said there was no zoning in the PDP only to say zoning was "alive and kicking" after Goodluck Jonathan had "won" his party's nomination. The National Chairman of the PDP, Prince Vincent Ogbulafor, a southerner who reminded party members that the presidency belonged to the north for another 4 years, was promptly replaced.*

*The provisions of the national constitution favoured Goodluck Jonathan and he was, anyway, already president. However, the denial of an important party arrangement in a severely fragile nation may still be having its consequences. General Andrew Owoye Azazi, the National Security Adviser, attributed the escalation of tension in the northern part of Nigeria to the breach of that important party arrangement. The election of Jonathan in the April election was greeted with violence and rioting in the North.*

## History of Leadership crises

Even when we are not being dishonest, we tend to be either confused or too emotional about the leadership question. The Yoruba Council of Elders (YCE), while urging all political parties to drop their zoning policies, was reported in the Guardian of June 25, 2010 as calling on Nigerians to elect the next president from the South-South geo-political zone. Are these 'elders' not unwittingly arguing the case for the same zoning principle they want dropped by the political parties? How can they realistically achieve their sentiment of having the president come from a particular region when a multitude of contestants from other regions of the federation also seek the same position? With due respect, this call by the elders is one expression of confusion which one finds rather difficult to rationalize.

Equally confusing is the often vague talk of competence and meritocracy. These desirable attributes can be found in all the regions of the Nigerian federation where we can point at individuals who have excelled in various leadership positions. We can point at individuals who are good senators or good governors. Even then, the so-called 'best candidate' may not always win in a situation where all sorts of sentiments inform the voting decision of individuals.

The problem we are confronted with in Nigeria is that of cleavage which does not get resolved by preaching to people to forget about what they hold dear to their hearts. To say Nigeria can survive is a tactic way of admitting that Nigeria may not survive. The question of the survival of a nation would not be a matter of discussion if factors that can lead to its demise do not exist. The factors of different languages, contrasting culture and religion, could lead to the demise of a nation if, more significantly, they reside with nationalities whose territorial boundaries are also exclusive. Ethnicity and religion will not disappear, but we can create a peaceful environment for development and co-existence by devising ways of accommodating what we are not going to be able to change. The history of our nation, by virtue of the aforementioned differences, has been one in which the leadership question has equally been the national question. If we are honest, it is one question we can deploy our collective wisdom to resolving. The Civil War of 1967-70 was the first time ever that the continued existence of Nigeria as one nation was violently contested. There were remote as well as immediate causes for that unfortunate war. The remote causes can be traced to the colonial divisive approach to political governance, a structural imbalance in which political power skewed in favour of one regional grouping to the detriment of others. The 50% electoral representation which the North secured at the Ibadan Constitutional Conference of 1950 placed it in an advantageous position over the East and the West. The military coup d'état of January 15, 1966, spearheaded by officers of southern origin was, in most interpretations, an attempt to redress an imbalance which politicians of their own regions had been unable to achieve. The counter-coup of July 29 1966, spearheaded by officers of northern origin, restored Nigeria to what was then the status quo ante.

The Gideon Orkar-led attempted coup of April 1990 was another occasion for a violent challenge to what had become northern primacy in national politics. The political style of General Ibrahim Babangida accounted for the revolt. The understandably angry coupists announced the suspension of key northern states from the federation, as they also rubbished the person of General Ibrahim Babangida as derogatorily as they possibly could. Even those of us outside the military barracks had cause to wonder if the south had become a colony of the north. General Babangida's cabinet reshuffle of December 1989 in which key portfolios went to the north while less attractive ones fell to the south prompted this writer, among other disenchanted Nigerians of southern origin, to openly dispute the honesty of General Babangida. The much wider crisis that would later come with his annulment of the presidential election of June 12, 1993, presumably won by a politician from the south, did vindicate our perception of his dishonesty. That annulment, soon followed by the tyranny of General Sani Abacha, encouraged the rise of ethnic militias making claims for regions whose interests had become rather antagonistic of one another.

The one good thing that came out of the June 12 crisis was that the leadership question which most of us would rather grumble about became a matter for open discussion. We urged for the rotation of the presidency between geo-political zones, and by "we" this writer means our politicians from the south of the Nigerian federation. The General Sani Abacha gimmick constitution of 1995 formally introduced the principle of leadership rotation between the North and South; however, the principle was informally adopted by the ruling Peoples Democratic Party (PDP) when the beautiful game of democracy supplanted military dictatorship in 1999. General Olusegun Obasanjo became the first beneficiary of that principle, a truth that must not be allowed to drown in the ocean of current emotions.

The principle, imperfect as it is, would appear to have reasonably stabilized our otherwise divided nation in the last 10 years. It can be improved upon, those calling for the principle of zoning and the allied "federal character" to be expunged, do not seem to appreciate the chaos of a history that could soon repeat itself. The noises about the direction of the presidency in 2011 should remind us that our nation is not divided by ideology, but by religion, region and selfish interests. It will suffice to repeat here that nations differ in their origins and complexities. The founding fathers of America did not have Nigeria in mind while designing their political arrangement, what we urgently need in Nigeria is a Nigerian political system.

*The Guardian, 01 July 2010*

# Zoning: The dishonesty in us

THIS writer confronted the government of General Ibrahim Babangida with two memoranda in the 1980s. The first had to do with reducing the cost of governance. The writer argued the case for the reduction of senatorial seats from five to three per state, not least because the number of states had increased from 19 in the Second Republic to 30 during the rule of General Babangida. While not claiming that this viewpoint influenced the outcome of their decision, it nevertheless complimented it.

The second memorandum was on the issue of leadership rotation which, not surprisingly, has now assumed topical dimensions. The idea of "zoning" began with the formation of the National Party of Nigeria (NPN) in 1978; it became more popular in the aftermath of the annulment of the presidential election of June 12, 1993. This writer was among the first generation of Nigerians to take the case for a rotational presidency to the pages of newspapers, journals and books. The article this writer wrote in The Guardian of June 7, 1985, "Towards the Third Republic: Zoning Revisited" was soon followed by that of Lt. General Theophilus Danjuma early in 1986, arguing along similar lines. The argument for zoning to be entrenched in the national constitution was not accepted by the Political Bureau but it is credit to that viewpoint that General Babangida himself is today one advocate of zoning.

Human beings can be dishonest when it comes to matters of selfish interest. The prospect that the presidency would rotate between regions helped the spread of support in the south of the otherwise northern-dominated NPN. Following the annulment of the presidential election of June 12, 1993, support for rotational presidency grew considerably in the south. Support for the idea has now shifted dramatically to the north, not least because the presidency of Goodluck Jonathan has armed the south with the assumption that the ball in their court could remain where it is. Consequently, ambitious politicians of the People's Democratic Party (PDP) from the north find themselves in an unusual corner, literally having to be begging their southern counterparts that the zoning "agreement" should be respected.

The chairman of the PDP, Dr. Okwesilieze Nwodo was recently reported as having pronounced zoning as an idea that died in 1999, not least because of its breach by members of the party. However, the chairman who was perhaps the most recent beneficiary of the party's zoning principle was soon made to deny the report. He now says the zoning principle would be revisited.

Such a possible revisit could have been motivated by no other reason other than an anxiety to accommodate the yet-to-be declared intention of incumbent President Goodluck Jonathan to contest the 2011 presidential election. Dr. Jonathan succeeded the late president, Alhaji Umaru Musa Yar'Adua who died in office on May 5, 2010. Had the latter not died and had been of good health, debate on the zoning principle might not have assumed its current topicality. Some commentators in the south would now argue that God has zoned the presidency to Goodluck Jonathan whose presumed intention to continue as president beyond May 2011 must not be challenged. However the bitter truth is that if what befell Yar'Adua had befallen General Olusegun Obasanjo, say about 2002, the position in the north would have been equally "selfish". It would probably have been politicians from the south reminding northern counterparts that an arrangement had to be respected!

Of course the "revisit" hinted at by Dr. Nwodo might also be intended to fortify the zoning principle constitutionally and make it binding on members. It could also be intended to expunge it altogether. Whatever happens to the zoning philosophy of the PDP in the days or months ahead, zoning is one idea that may not go away. To want to do away with zoning or "federal character" could be like attempting to run away from one's own shadow. The ethnological realities of our society make it imperative that we engage in a "balancing act" for the sake of its survival. The United States of America did the same in bringing small and large states together, hence the introduction of a bi-camera legislature. What we must quickly understand in Nigeria is that a nation cannot run away from its history and political realities.

Perhaps the reason other political parties are not engulfed in the zoning debate is because the presidential candidacies of most of the parties are already "zoned" to the ambitions of their "owners". It was, for instance, highly predictable that General Muhammadu Buhari would not be part of the zoning controversy in the north, principally because anything other than he himself being a presidential candidate would have been unthinkable!

It is amazing how people have been confusing themselves on the contentious issue of zoning. Even those calling for the idea to be jettisoned have no qualms advocating at the same time that the next president be elected from their own region. One would have thought that anyone opposed to the zoning of the presidency wouldn't be bothered about where the president comes from. Some assume that zoning encourages mediocrity but is it not an acknowledgement of the reality of our society that no Yoruba person has shown an active interest in the presidency since General Olusegun Obasanjo, a Yoruba, left office in 2007? Would it have mattered much in a less divided society that a child succeeds his or her own parent as president?

The great constitutionalist, Professor Ben Nwabueze, has competently diagnosed the leadership problem in Nigeria as a psychological one. It is not the president that should be blamed if, for instance, a child does not get a place in school or college. There are other layers of government, local and state, responsible for matters that touch on our daily existence. The leadership problem is about our unity and the continued existence of our nation as an indivisible entity. A more honest people will take a hard look at the history of their nation as well as the sentiments of its peoples and work out a political arrangement that douses tension. A nation can decide its own structure of democracy.

*The Guardian, 15 July 2010*

# Jonathan and the future of Zoning

Congratulations to President Goodluck Jonathan on securing the nomination of his party, the Peoples Democratic Party, in the recently concluded party primaries. Jonathan need not be reminded that he would now have to embark on reconciling aggrieved members of his party, if his ambition of becoming an elected president in 2011 is to be realised.

The victory of Dr. Goodluck Jonathan was believed to have been facilitated by governors who exercised some kind of control over state delegates. In a more sophisticated political environment where individuals have full control over the choices they make, the PDP primaries might have revealed a more competitive outcome.

Some governors, overzealous as they were in their support for Jonathan, would not even allow his main rival, Alhaji Atiku Abubakar, to speak to delegates in their states. This type of overzealousness does not speak for democracy and should be roundly condemned. The concerned governors have behaved like idiots and zealots, forgetting to realise that a time may come in their political careers when they themselves could be seeking support beyond their narrow territories.

Primaries are exclusive to political parties and their outcome may not necessarily reflect the quality of support on the ground. While governors might have succeeded in getting delegates to smile all the way from Abuja to the banks, the task of helping Goodluck Jonathan to continue in his job beyond May 2011 would be in convincing the larger voting public about the rightness of his choice. Confronted by an election that promises to be decided overwhelmingly by sentiments, the task can hardly be an easy one.

The victory or otherwise of Goodluck Jonathan in the April presidential election would speak loudly for the future of Zoning and Rotation- positively, of course. The ingenuous idea of zoning and rotation - an idea supported by this writer-was conceived to give the most realistic advantage to members of the minority ethnic group in a political system dominated by those of the so-called majority ethnic groups. There is, therefore, a sense in which the presidency of Goodluck Jonathan, a member of the former, is celebrated warmly by proponents and supporters of this idea.

It should not be easily forgotten that Goodluck Jonathan rode on the platform of zoning to be what he is today. Even when his ardent supporters would want to rubbish zoning, we knew they were doing so in desperation. For it would have been a major contradiction for them to justify zoning while at the same time insisting on the candidacy of Goodluck Jonathan. The PDP leadership might have been dishonest in its double talk on zoning, but that is the nature of politics in a society whose politicians love democracy but resent the rules and principles that give meaning to it. However, should Jonathan be elected in April, it might be difficult to resist the pressure for the presidency to shift to either the North or South- East in 2015.

The defeat of President Goodluck Jonathan in April, in the event that it does happen, would still justify the relevance of zoning. Apart from the fact that the dishonesty in handling the zoning controversy might have produced disenchanted members of the PDP who would want to vote against their party in the presidential election, such a possible defeat could also mean that the ambition of Jonathan was crushed by the superior force of ethnicity. For without any attempt to be disrespectful to those who would want to be presidential candidates in April, the projection we already have here is that of a three horse race. If any candidate is going to snatch the presidential baton from Jonathan, that candidate would possibly be Muhammadu Buhari of the Congress for Progressive Change or Nuhu Ribadu of the Action Congress of Nigeria. They are both members of a majority ethnic group of the North and their challenge is credible. Other presidential aspirants would appear to be merely making up the numbers or keeping up appearances.

Post PDP era, if it does happen in May, should be quite interesting A new political party in power would in a matter of time come to the realisation that zoning is to Nigeria what butter is to bread. Zoning will not go away for as long as the system we have is the presidential one. In the final analysis it might be in the national interest that zoning be formalized in order to make it constitutionally binding on all. Zoning is undoubtedly that thread that holds divided Nigeria together.

This article is dedicated to the memory of my great friend, Dr Tajudeen Abdul-Raheem who would have been 50 on January the 6th. A great scholar and committed Nigerian nationalist with whom I enjoyed spirited debates on political issues, he was born on the 6th of January 1961 and died on the 25th of May 2009.

*The Guardian, 15 July 2010*

# Being Wary of Their "Luck"

If rising to the pinnacle of political power is considered to be luck, then it is highly debatable who has been the luckier between General Olusegun Obasanjo and incumbent President Goodluck Jonathan. The latter became president in less than twelve years of involvement in partisan politics, reputed never to have mounted the podium to seek electoral votes on behalf of himself. Jonathan's rise to the top has been meteoric and the more religious ones among us would interpret it as the design of powers beyond human understanding.

Dr Jonathan became Governor of Bayelsa State following the impeachment of his kleptocratic boss and, later, president of the Nigerian federation because the one elected into that position died while in office. He had been deputy governor and vice-president in both instances. There can be no doubt that Jonathan has been lucky and any parent would be understood if they chose to name their child "Goodluck" in the hope that that name brings good fortune!

In spite of Goodluck Jonathan's seemingly legendary luck, my vote for the luckier candidate would go to General Olusegun Obasanjo, for the simple reason that his luck had been tested. General Obasanjo was not the most accomplished commander during the Nigerian Civil War of 1967-70, yet the historic encomium went to him not least because he accepted the surrender of the then rebels! He became military leader and head of state following the assassination of his boss, General Murtala Mohammed in 1976 and went on to be elected president in 1999, having been dragged from the death den of General Sani Abacha. The world admired him because, in 1979, he demonstrated commitment to principles by handing over voluntarily to an elected government. His sceptics would, however, say he had no choice.

General Obasanjo celebrates his luck in books, My Command and Not My Will, as well as in a document, "From Prison to Presidency". The book, Not My Will takes a swipe at Chief Obafemi Awolowo, arguably the most disciplined and prepared politician, who sought the political leadership of Nigeria thrice and was denied his aspiration on each occasion. Obasanjo's luck has also not failed to rub off on his chosen ones!

It could be argued that the late President Umaru Musa Yar'adua might still be alive today if not for the rigours of office. His health might not have deteriorated badly if he had had a relatively restful life. The philosophical counter to that argument would be that Yar'adua nevertheless achieved what many would only dream about. To be a leader of one's own nation is perhaps the greatest honour history can bestow on any individual. It is only idiots who perceive leadership as an opportunity for self-enrichment.

General Obasanjo single-handedly elevated Umaru Yar'adua to the enviable position of president; he did it for his great friend and ally, the late General Shehu Yar'adua who died in suspicious circumstances while in Abacha's detention camp. He probably also did it in the selfish assumption that Umaru Yar'adua would be there for him to manipulate. Umaru Yar'adua won the 2007 presidential election which General Obasanjo codified as "do or die".

General Olusegun Obasanjo has also been instrumental in propelling Dr Goodluck Jonathan to his exulted position of president. It was Obasanjo who influenced the choice of Jonathan as running mate to Umaru Yar'adua in the 2007 election. If Jonathan were to be elected as president in 2011, the Obasanjo magic would undoubtedly be a factor in it. The contentious zoning debate was sparked off by General Obasanjo's dishonest denial of the existence of zoning as the driving philosophy of his People's Democratic Party (PDP), not least because of the anxiety to accommodate the presumed ambition of Jonathan to continue in office beyond May 2011.

General Obasanjo has now come out, all guns blazing, in support of Jonathan for the presidency. His war song, reminiscent of the disgraceful "do or die" battle cry on behalf of the deceased Umaru Yar'adua, is now the equally contemptible "Operation totality".

One would have assumed that General Obasanjo, as Chairman of the PDP's Board of Trustees (BOT) would wait patiently for the party's primaries to be concluded before throwing his weight behind whoever emerges as the presidential candidate of the party. Of course, we have our preferences but certain positions call for discretion and neutrality even if pretentious, in the behaviour of "exalted" individuals. General Obasanjo has characteristically not exercised that discretion or neutrality and his party could pay dearly for it in 2011.

Maybe PDP's dominance is deservedly coming to a halt, as President Muhammadu Buhari waits patiently in the wings to sort their mess out! Were it not for the pressure from Obasanjo and co, Goodluck Jonathan was honest enough to acknowledge that the presidential candidacy of the ruling PDP still belongs to the North. He was humble enough to have indicated that reverting to his erstwhile position of vice president would not be beyond his contemplation. Jonathan would appear to be driven against himself; it would require the exceptional courage of a highly principled and disciplined mind to be able to scorn the wave of sycophancy, opportunism and, of course, genuine expectation, that cluster around his personage.

Our dishonesty has been overheating the polity, threatening to turn what should ordinarily be an exercise in democracy into a possible show of strength between the North and South. One continues to read of politicians advocating "southern solidarity" for Goodluck Jonathan, as one also reads about the possibility of the North presenting a "consensus candidate" to douse Jonathan's ambition. There can be only one outcome in the war of the cleavages - violence. There is this saying by our elders that when everything seems to be working for an individual, there is also the need for caution and sombre reflection - that warning could be meant for those of us who assume that our "luck", even when unmerited, is licence for arrogance and overbearing posturing.

*The Guardian, 26 August 2010*

# The Triumph of sentiments

The 2011 presidential election has been generally acknowledged as a massive improvement on previous ones and who else to identify for praise other than Professor Attahiru Jega (and his team), the Chairman of the Independent National Electoral Commission (INEC), who has approached this assignment with meticulous planning.

Dr Attahiru Jega has demonstrated patriotism and integrity, thereby justifying the nice things my late friend, Dr Tajudeen Abdul-Raheem said about him while introducing us about twenty years ago. President Goodluck Jonathan also deserves our commendations for it was he who appointed Jega to his position and would appear to have given him a free hand.

The 2011 presidential election itself, and this has nothing to do with Professor Jega per se, can be described as the convergence of sentiments and emotions that produced various electoral outcomes. In a more sophisticated political environment, and if the groaning of Nigerians was anything to go by, the ruling People's Democratic Party (PDP) no matter the humility and niceness of its presidential candidate, would have been made to say a temporary goodbye to the presidency for its rascality in political governance. Its leadership would have been asked to go and learn how to behave before being granted another chance. The PDP leadership has been corrupt and clueless, with nothing to show for the trillions of naira in national income. The PDP won the presidency for the fourth time of asking in as many elections, and who needs an elaborate explanation this time round when the name of the PDP presidential candidate is Goodluck.

Luck, be it good or bad, is a phenomenon which defies rational explanation. The 2011 presidential election may have been free and fair but the absence of rationality in our collective voting behaviour is one thing that will continue to worry the neutral. The volume of money injected into the process of corrupting the voter must also continue to worry us and that, in itself, questions the assumption that the presidential election may have been as free and fair as people are made to believe.

Be that as it may, the 2011 presidential election is a victory of some sort to our collective primordial sentiments, more than anything else. There are not just a few states where more than 90% of the electoral votes went to the "ethnic" candidate. Most of the states in the South-South and South-East geo-political zones, for understandable reasons, voted en masse for Goodluck Jonathan. The South-West geo-political zone is assumed to have become the bastion of support for the Action Congress of Nigeria (ACN); its presidential candidate, Malam Nuhu Ribadu, must be bemoaning his luck of having to be involved in an election at a time when the tsunami effect of Jonathanism had become unstoppable. Most people who would normally have voted ACN voted for the candidate of the PDP, Dr Goodluck Jonathan, for reasons not unconnected with him being the main southern candidate seeking the presidency against formidable northern rivals. Of course in most of the northern states, ethno-religious sentiments and intra-ethnic squabbling determined the direction of votes for either the main northern candidate, Major-General Muhammadu Buhari of the Congress for Progressive Change (CPC), or Goodluck Jonathan. Party-ism and the perception of personalities did play some part but such considerations would appear to have become the exception in the 2011 elections.

Of course our peoples must put the acrimonies and disappointments of the 2011 presidential election behind them and support Goodluck Jonathan in the assumption that he can succeed where his predecessors had failed woefully. Nigeria is the only major oil-producing nation of the world where the supply of electricity has been an issue for decades. Monies that should have gone into the development of our infrastructures, education system, health and other mundane aspects of human existence have disappeared into the pockets of perennial political termites in the corridors of power. President Goodluck Jonathan is acknowledged for humility but he will need more than that to succeed as president of the Federal Republic of Nigeria. A great leader is one that is confident, decisive and purposeful. Dr Jonathan must be prepared to fight the war against corruption because corruption is the single factor which has held our nation back since independence in 1960. Goodluck Jonathan has not been all that convincing in his almost one year of leadership; maybe being an elected president would now arm him with the courage that goes with effective leadership. Dr. Jonathan was like a timid boxer forced into the ring by hardened promoters, but he must now find the courage to engage in the contest proper.

One congratulates our compatriots who have been marginalised in our electoral calculations. Once there was a time in the life of our nation when a member of the minority ethnic group would not have been considered an electoral asset. The presidency was assumed to be the exclusive preserve of the majority ethnic group, particularly that of the north. This writer is proud to say he was one of those who vigorously challenged that assumption by arguing for a system based on leadership rotation in our type of divided society. Goodluck Jonathan is where he is today via the route of the vice-presidential candidate of his Party, the PDP zoned to the South-South geo-political zone in 2007. We should not be dishonest about the relevance of "zoning" and "rotation" because the sentiments and emotions that conspired in producing Goodluck Jonathan as an elected president have merely confirmed that we have been right all along. The politics of our nation will never be based on issues until we have found a way of cross-cutting our cleavages of ethnicity and religion.

It will be dishonest not to acknowledge that the strategic importance of the South-South geo-political zone as the region that accounts for our nation's wealth has rubbed off in the historic achievement of Goodluck Jonathan. Jonathan's first name may be about luck but it is doubtful if there would have been much support for him to "continue" with the mandate originally given to the late President Umaru Musa Yar'adua via the zoning arrangements of his party if he had been a Vice-president from elsewhere. The fear of what could happen to oil production in the event of him being denied the presidency was emphatically amplified by his campaigners in every nook and cranny of society. It can be argued that there is now  what can be called a "national consensus" in the relevance of a rotational presidency and that is what one would be admonishing Goodluck Jonathan about after he has been sworn into office in May. He himself has expressed support for the idea of a "one-term" presidency, which is to say we belong in the same camp.

*The Punch, 21 April 2011*

# Jonathan's Single term proposal

I write on the single-term proposal as one who believes in its necessity, even as one is equally aware that politicians can be dishonest. President Goodluck Jonathan's proposal of a single, six year tenure for president and governor is not seminal. but significant nevertheless. The idea of a single-term enjoys informed opinion and was in fact forcefully presented to the Political Bureau established by the military government of General Ibrahim Babangida in 1986. General Olusegun Obasanjo, one honest critic of the politics of the Second Republic (1979-1983) specifically suggested a single-term of six years to the Body.

The Political Bureau identified with the informed views of many Nigerians regarding the desirability of a single-term presidency in the context of the history and ethnological realities of our nation but the military leadership rejected their recommendations of a single-term of five years in favour of the existing two-terms of four years each. It is not as if the recommendation of the Political Bureau would have mattered; the transition engineered by the then military regime led to nothing!

Be that as it may, the idea of a single-term executive – once or twice approved by the legislative arm of government – continues to be trumpeted by individuals and groups. A group of well-informed and well-meaning Nigerians, The Patriots, amplified the idea as did also members of the Nigerian Bar Association (NBA) – in the early years of the current Republic. The proposal by President Goodluck Jonathan calls for thorough debate, not least because of its importance to our democracy and our nation. Of course this proposal may not be the most pressing issue of the moment.

The length of time a political leader spends in office is important. We in Africa know what its pernicious consequences could be, as elected leaders are transformed into monarchs of some sort. Presidential tenure has not been the most contentious issue in the United States of

America whose constitutional arrangements inform ours. Until Franklin Delano Roosevelt, elected president in 1932, it was always assumed that the American president was conventionally limited to two terms in office. However, Roosevelt was the only American President to have spent more than two terms in office; he died in 1945 during his fourth term. His successor, Harry S Truman, established the Hoover Commission in 1947 to look into the prospect of presidential term limits. The outcome was the 22nd Amendment of 1951 which limited the American President to two terms, or a maximum of 10 years where a President had started off by completing the tenure of another. The idea of a one term presidency was however seriously considered in the aftermath of the Watergate scandal.

The two term presidency is rationalised in political or academic argument. It is argued that a second term ensures that a hardworking President has enough time to complete his or her programmes. It also serves the purpose of rewarding hard work, as the less successful President is replaced after a term in office. These arguments resonate in Nigeria, even when native wisdom should inform us that the nature of one's political environment is the most important consideration in all of this. The political arrangement of Switzerland, the second oldest written constitution after the USA , comes to mind here.

The fact that one has been limited to a single term in office would not mean that he or she would embrace non-performance as a policy. Every individual wants to be remembered for something. In any case there is always a mechanism – impeachment, for instance, by which a pathetic President can be removed from office. There is also the political party machinery which will not go to sleep while its candidate messes up its prospects in a future election. The single-term presidency is not without its checks and balances!

This writer has himself been one advocate of a single-term executive; here are the extracts from the arguments he once advanced in support of this idea "… firstly, when the Executive is not in a position to seek re-election, there will be little or no inducement to use the instrument of state to facilitate electoral fraud. This is to say that the President would be wary of any scandal that could tarnish the reputation of his administration... secondly, the President would be induced to devote more of his attention to office, rather than dissipate energy over the question of re-election. It is common knowledge that a reasonable part of the first term is devoted to seeking re-election."

Thirdly, the President would be more of a father figure advancing the national interest to secure a place for himself in history. He may have been elected on the platform of a particular party, he can nevertheless afford to be non-partisan in certain circumstances ... finally, a one-term provision could not but be reasonable in Nigerian society where the ethno-regional origin of the national leader would for a very long time be a major issue. It would be hypocritical not to acknowledge this (see Anthony Akinola, *Rotational Presidency* (1996), pp 56-57)".

The proposal by President Goodluck Jonathan should not be disregarded because of a history of leadership dishonesty. His spokesman, Dr Reuben Abati, has told us that the proposal does not seek to have a retroactive effect. It will take effect from 2015, after which Dr Goodluck Jonathan will have vacated office based on his self-proclaimed determination to serve a term of four years only.

If this is the case, the law makers do not lack the knowledge of how they can craft an amendment that would give meaning to it. In fact, the proposal should be blended with the principle of "rotation", ensuring that the presidency shifts to another region of the Nigerian federation in 2015. The leadership question remains the Nigerian national question, we saw this in the violent reactions to the presidential election in April 2011. It is the responsibility of the Nigerians of today to seek to resolve the problems of their time.

*The Guardian, 01 August 2011*

# For single term rotational presidency

Political colonization may have ended with independence fifty years ago but the legacy of twisted thoughts it inflicted on us will persist.. Otherwise we would not be pre-occupied with some exotic format, which the two-term presidency can represent, while the reality of serious ethnic and religious divisions stares us in the face. Those who have warned or predicted that Nigeria could disintegrate by the year 2015 know what our "weakest links" are. They also know that the political class lacks focus and may not be patriotic or determined enough to chart a new course for the future.

The history of our nation would reveal that we have tempted "political fate" on quite a few occasions. Let us take a honest look at the Civil War of 1967-70; the Gideon Orkar-led attempted coup of April, 1990; the "June 12" crisis of 1993 – 1998, and, of course, the lingering post-election crisis of April 2011. Either directly or indirectly, these crises emanated from inter-ethnic rivalry for leadership position in a most divided nation. Of course, we are entitled to indulge ourselves in describing the election of Goodluck Jonathan as a "pan-Nigerian" mandate. The neutral would not buy into this over-exaggeration, as there is hardly anything pan-Nigerian in an election that pitched one section of society against another, with primordial sentiments running riot.

Dr. Jonathan feels the tensions he has had to contend with. He knows, even though the Constitution does not bar him, that a second- term in office would be difficult to negotiate. Would his "backers" still be able to argue that he is seeking to complete the "joint ticket" he held with the late Umaru Musa Yar'adua? It is in this sense that one is not in serious doubt that a patriotic Jonathan would honour his pledge to serve only one-term of 4 years and quit office in 2015. The contradictions of the Nigerian state- severe ethnic and religious divisions – also serve as checks and balances to "sit-tightism" in leadership position. Ask General Olusegun Obasanjo about this!

The assumption that Goodluck Jonathan would be honourable has encouraged one to want to re-emphasise the importance of the single term proposal vis-à-vis the stability of the Nigerian state. It must be quickly warned here that even when this proposal may not be the most pressing issue at this point in time, the stability of our nation will always be. We are not going to be able to legislate out of existence the rivalry and competition that go with the diversity of different peoples; however, we should be talented enough to be able to tame their consequences.

Other than question his integrity, there has not been any convincing argument articulated against Jonathan's single-term proposal. Those who assume that the elected president would merely bring his or her bed into office and snore away should know that a putative single-term presidency would not be unique to Nigeria. Mexico has a single-term of six years for president while Switzerland, for ethnological reasons not too dissimilar to ours, operates a collective presidency in which the leadership position is rotated yearly. Both nations are successful in many respects.

In the typical Nigerian way of viewing things, there is this expected intrusion of North-South parochialism in the debate. That, in itself, is to say that the political arrangement of any nation cannot be explained outside of the overall quality of its electorate. There are those who say Jonathan's proposal cannot be accepted by the North because the South has dominated the leadership space in recent years. Whereas their counterparts in the South will also want to emphasise the cumulative advantage of the North in this respect since independence in 1960. These types of sentiments do not speak for the purposefulness of a nation that is prepared to break with the past and face the future with determination.

President Jonathan's proposal will have to accommodate the principle of leadership rotation along defined constituencies for it to achieve the most important objective of national cohesion and stability. There is a sense in which we can say that this principle enjoys nationwide consensus. The South has always wanted it in spite of the opportunistic denial engendered by the wave of Jonathanism in the run-up to the presidential election of April 2011. The North insisted on it then and, recently, General Ibrahim Babangida was quoted as having rightly said that Nigeria could not do without "zoning".

The thing about zoning or the principle of rotation is that it can only work effectively in the context of a single-term format; it makes no sense with two terms. Why, for instance, would a given region whose turn it is to produce the president want its candidate to be re-elected? To put it differently, why would a region want to put itself in a position of possibly producing two presidents, each serving a term of 4 years, before another region could take its turn?

Let us conclude this essay by stating some lesson in constitutional democracy. The constitution of any democratic nation should be geared towards resolving the problem of the moment. When a condition that necessitates a provision in a given constitution no longer exists, that provision gets amended to accommodate new realities. That should be the way forward for Nigeria if its survival is indeed a priority of the moment.

*The Punch, 23 August 2011*

# PART 5

# ELECTIONS, PARTIES AND QUALIFICATIONS

## SYNOPSIS

*Nigeria has had about 12 years of uninterrupted democracy since 1999, the longest in consistency since independence from Great Britain in 1960. The political parties are still mostly ethnic-based and promises of politicians rather pedestrian. However there is the optimism that the continuity of the democratic order could create space for political maturity and leadership recruited on the bases of verifiable achievements. The methodologies of election and electioneering are worrying, and would need to improve considerably in the future.*

## Being President of Nigeria

There are not just a few individuals who should be thinking of where they would like to be buried but are still parading themselves as authentic political leaders and the future of the African continent! Robert Mugabe of Zimbabwe who is about 87 is rumoured to be plotting "re-election" in 2012! One can compare and contrast Africa's rule by the aged with other democratic nations of the world where political leadership has become more or less the exclusive preserve of energetic men and women in their forties and early fifties. Africa's dilemma in this regard is quite evident in its lack of comparative progress, but the concept of "generational change" in politics should not in itself be an imitation, but a development that comes with the establishments of democratic culture generally.

When we make comparisons between different societies, it is important that we do not take things at face value. It is attractive for anyone who argues for a generational change in political leadership in

Nigeria, for instance, to point at Great Britain where Prime Minister David Cameron is only 43, or the United States of America where Barack Obama is 49. A more critical evaluation of leadership in Britain and the United States of America in particular should focus on the grooming of the individual for the role he or she would later play in life.

Not least because of factors not unconnected with their stage of educational, political and economic development, children in some societies tend to achieve maturity much earlier than in others. In Great Britain, for example, the age of consent is 16. When a child has attained the legal age of consent, he or she becomes responsible for their omissions and commissions. At 18, a child is assumed to have become 'independent' of parents. By 21, it would be in exceptional or curious circumstances that one would still want to live under the same roof as one's parents. Parents in Britain do demand and collect rent from children of working age who choose to live at home.

The British society is so structured that when a child tells you of his or her age it would be more than mere guesswork to know exactly what stage of education he or she has attained. It is an age group thing; those who have chosen to go to university would have started their degree programmes at the age of 18 and finished by 21. Those of them who, for instance, want to go into politics choose relevant subjects for that call. At Oxford and Cambridge, for instances, future politicians are most likely to be studying Politics, Philosophy and Economics (PPE) or Law. Most identify with political parties based on viewpoints and they do voluntary or paid work in heir local constituencies particularly at election time. They imbibe the culture of rigorous debating during their apprenticeship. Your degree in biology or zoology, even when at the doctoral level, may not have prepared you adequately for a career in politics!

The point one is trying to make here is that the David Camerons and Barack Obamas of this world made their choices quite early in life. Even though David Cameron of Great Britain may be only 43, his experience in politics could have been that of about 20 or more years. The suitability or otherwise of a candidate for a leadership position becomes important from records of past behaviour. The type of company you keep at school, and that marijuana that you may have smoked at a relatively innocent age could, surprisingly, be an electoral issue that comes to haunt you in later life. So, there is an element of parental grooming in all of this!

President Barack Obama knew very early in life what he was aiming at. Even at a very early age he told one of his teachers that he wanted to be president of the United States. Prior to becoming state senator at Illinois and first-term senator in Congress, he had engaged himself in various community activities. His books spoke clearly for his future intentions. One is still looking around for that book in which any of our presidential aspirants may have told us about his or her background and their vision of society.

The general poverty in what one would want to call 'foundational grooming' suggests we, including our president, lack a capacity to engage counterparts elsewhere in coherent articulation of economic and political issues. Our politics exists at the elementary stage where issues, which other nations take for granted, still predominate political discussions- water, electricity, roads etc.

President Goodluck Jonathan, still learning on the job, has been demonstrating this preparatory inadequacy since the inception of his presidency, to the amusement of political rivals who are hardly better than he is in that respect. He makes critical decisions based on disjointed comments written on his 'Facebook'; he talks first, and thinks later, as suggested by the controversy surrounding the bomb blast at Abuja on Independence Day. If he needed to talk at all about the contentious zoning policy of his party, he probably should have attempted to corroborate his argument with those of his key supporters, even when dishonest, that he was seeking to serve out the joint mandate he held with the late President, Umaru Musa Yar'Adua. It was not tidy enough for him to have denied outright the zoning of the presidency by his party.

There are rivals of his who assume they can possibly 'sleepwalk' into the presidency in 2011, based on the hype surrounding their over-exaggerated importance or relevance in Nigerian politics. One would have thought that credentials of previous experience at some governmental level would matter for anyone wanting to be president of one of the most complex nations of the world. A serious candidate for president would seek to have a good understanding of his or her political environment, and this includes the psychology of those one would be sharing power with at the legislative and judicial arms of the government. In a more serious society, one's mere declaration of good intentions may not substitute for acquired experience in this regard.

Being a successful president of the Federal Republic of Nigeria is about being able to combine acquired wisdom with native intelligence. Most of our political leaders since independence have been relatively young individuals, so this generational shift many have been talking about seems misplaced if one must be honest. The real problem with our leadership has been the problem of inadequate preparation, integrity or purposefulness, and the experience of handling the manipulative influences of old hawks as well as those of sectional and vested interests- in the drive for what is good for us all.

*The Guardian 17 October 2010*

# Presidential debates in perspective

Even with the vast majority of Nigerians not having access to television and electricity, the culture of televised presidential debates has crept in and should be warmly embraced. It is one of the many cultures we have copied from the United States of America. The recently televised debate involving Major General Muhammadu Buhari of the Congress for Progressive Change (CPC), Malam Nuhu Ribadu of the Action Congress of Nigeria (ACN) and Malam Ibrahim Shekarau of the All Nigerian Peoples Party (ANPP), suggests it is one culture that is gradually taking root in our society. President Goodluck Jonathan, seeking to be elected into the position he occupies (he is not seeking re-election), did not participate in the debate organised by NN24. It will be revealed later in this article that such absence was not unusual, even in the United States of America.

It may interest students of political history to know that the first ever debate in the USA between rivals for elective, political office, can be traced to 1857 when Abraham Lincoln insisted on having a debate with Stephen Douglas on "the virtue of the republic and the evil of slavery". It was an unmoderated debate and what was then at stake was a senatorial seat in the State of Illinois. Abraham Lincoln lost that election but a history in political debating had already been made.

Abraham Lincoln would later win the presidency in 1860, in an election which featured no political debates. In fact, there were no debates between presidential candidates until 1952 when the League of Women Voters organised debates between presidential candidates. The culture of televised debate would later become formalised with the televised debate between John F. Kennedy and Richard Nixon in 1960. The handsome and more charismatic John Kennedy won the televised debate while an earlier radio debate had been won by Nixon. Mr Nixon was said to have appeared rather "shifty" on television and that contributed to his loss of the election.

If televised debates could prove the downfall of a candidate who otherwise could have won in an election, why bother to participate in them? President Lyndon Johnson refused to debate with Senator Barry Goldwater in 1964; he was leading in the polls, and public speaking was not his *forte*. Similarly in 1968 Richard Nixon who again contested the presidency with Senator George McGovern, refused to debate. Nixon was the front runner in the opinion polls and his non-participation might have been informed by his experience with John Kennedy in 1960.

Just as John McCain was about to do in one of his 2008 presidential debates when he said he was attending to legislative matters in Congress, President Jimmy Carter in 1980 refused to participate in the first presidential debate because it included independent candidate John Anderson. He, however, attended subsequent debates and that memorable question by Ronald Reagan did him great damage: "Are Americans better off today than they were four years ago?" The state of the economy and the American hostage crisis in Iran suggested it was the right question that would nail the coffin of the Carter presidency.

The official explanation for the absence of Goodluck Jonathan at the debate organised by NN24 was that he had committed himself to an engagement involving political leaders of other nations. It was as if the presidential debate was neither important enough nor pre-arranged. With no major achievement to flaunt in his one year of leadership and with all the ills associated with his political party – the Peoples Democratic Party (PDP) – the suggestion that Goodluck Jonathan might have "chickened out" could not be far-fetched:. Of course this should be seen if he does participate in a future debate. Lack of confidence in public speaking could be a factor that makes one not want to debate with opponents.

One did watch a recording of the debate organised by NN24 with some friends. "You can see that the man is talking sense" was one sentence that a Nigerian kept on repeating each time the candidate of his choice took the stage. He seemed not to see any sense in what other presidential candidates were saying! The lack of objectivity on the part of our peoples suggests that the real value in the Nigerian presidential debate still belongs to the distant future.

The essence of a presidential debate would be fully appreciated in a society where the people see it as an opportunity to evaluate the policies, preparedness and demeanour of those who seek to govern them. It must, however, also be warned that a great leader may not be the best of debaters.

In the United States of America where televised presidential debates have been around for 50 years, or in Great Britain where debates between potential prime ministers took off for the first time in 2010, the outcome of elections tends to be decided by those alluded to as "floating voters". This is more so in the United States of America where the outcome of a presidential election could be dramatically influenced by an event on voting day. The one portrayed as frontrunner could suddenly find himself or herself struggling to catch up in the opinion polls! We are not there yet!

Our contemporary political behaviour is informed by bigotry and primordial sentiments. It will take many years of education and improvements in the economic wellbeing of our peoples to overcome ethnic and religious bigotry. There is nothing particularly Nigerian in what one is saying here because overcoming bigotry has been an historical struggle even in the United States itself. Once there was a time in American history when a Barack Obama could not even have dreamt of walking near the lawns of the White House. Such a dream would have been interpreted as that of a black person about to be lynched!

Nigeria shall be a great nation and we as a people shall be where we deserve to be – in the comity of civilised peoples. Sadly, some of the leaders we have today – the so-called "His Excellencies" – have the natural dispositions of touts or thugs. Of what use would a political debate have been in a society where "new colonial masters" would decide on who and who not to canvass for political support in their "colonies". These so-called leaders are the misfortunes of our society because they do not lead our peoples to behave appropriately and democratically. Can the new culture of political debates achieve much in a culture of "do or die" politics? We shall get to where we want to be even when the journey is still long.

*The Guardian, 28 March 2011*

# Parties and the party system

This article is informed by a report in <u>The Guardian</u> of 7 January 2006 that "opposition parties" intend to co-operate in challenging the ruling People's Democratic Party (PDP) in the assumed presidential election of 2007. The Nigerian experience with both the parliamentary and presidential systems of government offers the astute student of comparative politics an opportunity to compare and contrast the influences of the political system on the development of political parties and the party system. While the parliamentary system tends to encourage the multiplicity of political parties, the presidential system tends to compel fusion.

From about 1952 to January 1966 when Nigeria experimented with the parliamentary system of government, small and large political parties remained important in their geographical areas of influence and depended on each other in the politics of alliances that were reminiscent of the era. For instance, the United Middle Belt Congress (UMBC) which advocated the creation of a Middle Belt Region out of the north, co-existed in a hostile relationship with the ethnocentric Northern People's Congress (NPC) while allying itself with the Yoruba-dominated Action Group (AG) which identified with its cause.

Nigeria opted for the American-type presidential system of government in 1979. The late Chief Obafemi Awolowo of the defunct Unity Party of Nigeria (UPN) was quick to grasp the realities of the new constitution vis-à-vis political parties. The 1979 elections were staggered into five different stages, with the presidential election coming last. Once Awolowo realised the NPN was the party to beat, he urged political parties in the so-called progressive family to co-operate in order to prevent the NPN from winning the presidency. Awolowo's "stop the NPN" clarion call was not heeded in 1979 but the NPN strategists realised its danger and used its influence to prevail on the Federal Electoral Commission to alter the pattern of elections by starting the 1983 arrangements with the presidential one.

The fact with the parliamentary system of government is that if no political party achieves a clear-cut majority in the outcome of elections, a small political party with just a few parliamentary seats could be pivotal to the formation of government. Whereas in a matured presidential system it is not absolutely crucial for the president's party to have the overwhelming majority of parliamentary seats. The point one is trying to make here is that the factors which decide who becomes a successful Prime Minister of Great Britain, for instance, may be quite different from those which decide that of the American President. The American Constitution provides for independent candidacy, not least because of the assumption that the President is above party and partisan influences.

The President exercises immense power, authority and influence, being the single occupant of the positions of Head of Government and Head of State, that most people want to belong to his or her political party. In a society with cleavage problems such as ours, that also explains why most people also want the presidency for their own group. The realisation that the presidency can only be won by a political party of sufficient strength explains why intelligent political strategists and actors would rather see mushroom political parties merge or fuse together in order to be able to counterbalance the power or power potential of a rival political party. The so-called Progressive Parties Alliance (PPA) failed to achieve its aspirations in the Second Republic (1979-1983) because ethnic and leadership rivalries were superior to the assumed progressive ideology of the member political parties.

A similar fate awaits the current opposition parties if the issue of national leadership is not boldly addressed in a new or amended Constitution. The problem of cleavage, be it that of ethnicity or religion, is the most serious of political problems. It is not a problem that can be resolved by preaching to people to forget about their religion or the aspirations of the group to which they belong. The nations whose constitutions we have experimented with, Britain and America, are quite different from our nation in terms of their origins and ethnological realities. The North of America may have produced more presidents than the South but the fact remains that the concepts of North and South hold different meanings for the American nation than they do for Nigeria. It is principally because nations differ from one another that there cannot be a unique, universal model of democracy for all to embrace.

The much-liked Alhaji Balarabe Musa assumes that what Nigerians refer to as "power-shift" has benefited no one (The Guardian, 7 January 2006). He is of the opinion that it is unpatriotic to advocate "rotational presidency" for Nigeria. It is not only that power-shift has helped some groups to become psychologically reconciled with the larger society, the truth of the matter is that President Olusegun Obasanjo, who probably would not have won a national election in 1999 but for the power-shift formula, has been head and shoulders above those predecessors of his who achieved positions of national leadership through hegemonic politics of some sort. Obasanjo may not be quite the "messiah" he assumed himself to be, there are nevertheless some ideas of development which can be associated with his name when, hopefully, he leaves office honourably in May 2007. The fight against corruption may be half-hearted and selective but a fight is still better than no fight at all. A less assuming political leader with democratic disposition and credentials can improve on things.

This article concludes with the assertion that the stability of our political parties and the emerging party system can only be guaranteed when our peoples feel a sense of belonging and have become loyal to the political order. While we may borrow ideas from some advanced nations in designing our political system, there can be no better or more useful ideas than the ones which derive from our own experiences as a people. It needs no reminding that every major crisis we have experienced in our nation has been associated with controversy over national leadership.

*The Guardian, 10 January 2006*

# Fusion, not party alliances

There is no serious ideological divide in Nigeria. What divides Nigerians is their ethnicity or religion. This notwithstanding, competitive political parties are desirable for effective governance. Political office holders will have more respect for the electorate if they realise that there is a credible alternative party on the ground ready to take over the reins of governance. The People's Democratic Party (PDP), detestable as it may be in the eyes of many, is currently the only political party better organised and relatively disciplined to manage the affairs of the Nigerian state. Others will have to organise to be able to provide the competition we so much desire in the polity.

There is some kind of a history of party development in Nigeria which is about "other parties" struggling to challenge the position of a relatively dominant one. In the First Republic, for instance, the Northern People's Congress (NPC) was the dominant party whose awesome control of the centre provoked the alliances of other political parties. A series of shifting alliances between parties culminated in grand alliances that aped a two-party competition. The 1964 Federal elections were contested between a group of politicians which styled themselves as progressive, the United Progressive Grand Alliance (UPGA), and another group assumed to be conservatives, the Nigerian National Alliance (NNA) which revolved around the ethnocentric NPC. The alliances collapsed with the demise of the First Republic in January 1966.

History repeated itself in the Second Republic (1979-1983) when the National Party of Nigeria (NPN) emerged as the relatively dominant political party following the 1979 elections, thereby compelling self-styled progressive politicians to attempt to forge an alternative political party via the Progressive Parties Alliance (PPA). The progressive politicians held a series of meetings and rallies, giving an impression that something great was going to happen. The alliance collapsed on the altar of ethnic politics as the members were unable to agree a common candidate for the 1983 presidential elections. However, they agreed to support in the presidential election whichever member of the alliance posed the greatest challenge to the NPN candidate – a strategy that met its waterloo once the electoral arrangement was reversed to begin with that of the president.

What would appear to be a blatant attempt to compel the fusion of the progressive and conservative ideological assumptions or tendencies in Nigerian politics came in the Third Republic when General Ibrahim Babangida decreed two political parties – the Social Democratic Party (SDP) and the National Republican Convention (NRC) – into existence. Sadly, General Babangida himself killed off his own experiment making it impossible for us to know how far it could have gone. However, the history of political party development here or in any other place suggests it was one experiment which in the long term hardly had any chance of succeeding. While a nation may choose to be a one-party state or a multi-party state, compartmentalising one as large and diverse as Nigeria into two political parties was indeed one hell of an experiment in political engineering.

General Babanbida's seeming aberration was soon followed by General Sani Abacha's joke of five political parties that would have a consensus presidential candidate which was to be himself. However, fate did not permit the Abacha joke to further infuriate our sensibilities and maybe we now know better that there is really no alternative to democracy in whatever shape it presents itself. The current shape of democracy in our society may not be the most ideal but democracy is nevertheless one experiment that improves with practice and continuity. The People's Democratic Party (PDP) urgently needs genuine rival political parties and not toothless and spineless opposition parties.

The dominance of the PDP is more or less a continuation of the tendencies witnessed in the First and Second Republics when the NPC and NPN respectively dominated the political space. The politics of alliances might have been suitable in the parliamentary system as practised in the First Republic when post-electoral coalitions between parties decided Government and Opposition but the presidential system of government is a different kettle of fish. Parties have to be

112

of sufficient strength to be realistically able to challenge for the presidency and that is why it is absolutely important for Nigeria's minor political parties to consider merging their forces rather than continuing to agonise about the PDP. This writer has argued consistently that truly competitive political parties that traverse ethnic and religious divides can emerge if the principle of leadership rotation is entrenched in the constitution. If the Nigerian Constitution is ever going to be reviewed, this position should be favourably considered as it is one effective way of removing the hob around which support for the ethnic political party revolves.

Helped by an electoral institution which is truly independent and fair to all parties, the people themselves are the most important elements in the trend and direction of a nation's party system. They are the ones who decide with their ballots whether or not a set of political office holders should continue to serve. One phenomenon in the old democratic nations, particularly America and Britain, is the continued increase in the number of independent or floating voters. They, not the traditional card-carrying supporters, decide the outcome of major elections. One believes strongly there would be a large number of such independent voters in the Nigerian society once major political parties have ceased to be ethnic.

It was said at the beginning of this article that Nigeria does not have a serious ideological divide and that should not suggest anything negative. The presidential system of government thrives on such an atmosphere. The absence of a serious ideological divide explains why America's two political parties, the Democratic Party and the Republican Party, have co-existed and worked for common good over the years. Where there is a serious ideological divide, one party might assume it had an obligation to silence the other whenever the opportunity presents itself. However, our elected politicians are enjoined to respect their mandates and stop prostituting themselves. Defecting from one political party to the other does not help the cause of a stable, competitive party system.

*The Guardian, 22 April 2009*

# Of Manifestos and Credible Candidacy

One James Boima Rogers, a Liberian scholar and good friend of mine, enthusiastically suggested that one take a comparative look at the manifestos of presidential aspirants with a view to determining their credibility. This suggestion is undoubtedly worthy but of what use is it in Nigeria where politicians still 'parrot' the same promises made by their predecessors 50 years ago? Are these candidates going to be saying anything different from one another? One assumes it serves a more useful purpose to merely remind politicians of their failed promises and, of course, repeat one's future expectations regardless.

Many societies of the world, including a few African nations, take the supply of electricity and running water for granted. Nigeria does not have that luxury, as promises of improvements in electricity and water supplies would feature prominently in the run-up to the 2011 elections. Politicians would promise on how they intend to provide good roads, functioning hospitals, quality education, jobs, security of life and property, among others. Nigerians are used to all these phony promises, the surprise can only come when they see them become a reality!

The inability of politicians to transform Nigeria into a modern society is not due to the unavailability of expertise but the culture of corruption and profligacy of politicians and public officials.

Nigeria is one of the most corrupt nations of the world, duly acknowledged so by the world community and Nigerians themselves. To its credit, the administration of erstwhile President Olusegun Obasanjo (1999-2007) established the Economic and Financial Crimes Commission (EFCC) in order to fight corruption and other related crimes in Nigerian society. It was the first time ever that corruption was highlighted as a serious issue in the polity; however, the meaningful results have yet to be achieved. The commission has more or less been a tool in the hands of political leadership to harass and frighten real and perceived enemies. Politicians have not become poorer because of investigations made into their conspicuous loots! Their arrogance has hardly been curtailed!!

The corruption and profligacy of politicians notwithstanding, the source of the nation's wealth- that source of politicians' greed- would need to be protected. However, the agricultural sector of the economy would also need to be revamped in order to reduce dependency on oil. Key politicians agree on the importance of doing more for the peoples of the Niger Delta region where most of the nation's oil is produced. Their words and promises must now translate into action if they genuinely intend to curtail possible tension arising from popular and organised action over environmental degradation, resulting from massive oil production. The peoples of that region have indeed been most patriotic and exceptionally tolerant. Things might have been different were the resources to be located elsewhere, in the territories of the so-called majority ethnic groups.

The long-term solution to this lopsided economic dependency would seem to be in transforming Nigeria into a true federal nation. The culture of sharing money at Abuja has the sad implication of not encouraging other component units of the Nigerian federation to develop their own possible sources of income. The erroneous assumption that meaningful development can take place without the people themselves making contributions in the form of taxation should be discouraged. If people are empowered by less corrupt governments that create wealth, they will hardly require much persuasion to the fact that individual contributions help the cause of a great society. Our so-called 'oil wealth' may not last forever.

The great Chinua Achebe said it all when he wrote that the problem with Nigeria is that of leadership. The leader that would ensure that the enormous wealth of Nigeria is used in developing Nigeria and its peoples would himself or herself be incorruptible. Such a political leader would take the fight against corruption as a personal commitment or a mission of life. He or she would be a political leader that has moral authority, someone who is seen to be practicing what he or she is preaching. Paying lip service to the fight against corruption will not do: corruption is that singular factor that has held

Nigeria back since independence in 1960. The ability and willingness to engage in the fight against corruption should be the most important factor that makes a presidential candidate credible or not in the 2011 election.

Sadly the 2011 presidential election promises, for several reasons, to be decided on the altar of sentiment. Even before candidates for the election were known to Nigerians there were lousy endorsements of individuals made here and there. One would have thought that a more purposeful people would have criteria for preferring one candidate to another. Even if there must be endorsements, should a collection of discredited and corrupt politicians insult their own people's sensibilities by making endorsements of selfish interest on their behalf?

Maybe there should be a television debate and maybe there should not be one. The argument for a possible television debate between presidential contestants is that it provides us with the opportunity to assess how prepared they are for the job they seek. The sceptic would, however, ponder the nature of the audience of such a debate. How many of them have not actually made up their minds on who they will be voting for in the April elections? To put it differently, how many Nigerians will remain as undecided voters until they have had the opportunity to listen to the various contestants and their arguments? What percentage of the Nigerian population has access to television or would be interested in a political debate?

It may therefore be reasonable to assume that political experience is, after all, the most crucial in all of this. While one does not have to have been president in order to be president, maybe the only way we can reasonably gamble our political future on any individual is our perception of how he or she performed in a previous political position. Taking an uninformed risk could be dangerous in a nation that is as volatile as ours. Maybe wanting to get to the top could also mean learning how to climb the ladder. It is all about patience and purposeful planning for the future. With patience, good luck can come!!!

*The Guardian 07 February 2011*

# Towards a more integrative party system

Referring to the political party that does not control the presidency as an "opposition party" is some kind of "hangover" from our experience with the parliamentary system of government. Under that system, a political party which has won the majority of seats in a parliamentary election forms the government, while the members of the one that has lost out are confined to the opposition benches. The parliamentary system is adversarial in approach and that in itself is deep-rooted in British political history.

Unlike the parliamentary system of government, the presidential alternative is a form of coalition government most suitable for a heterogeneous nation like ours. The responsibilities of government are shared between its three arms – the executive, legislative and judicial. The Americans who "invented" the presidential system we practise in Nigeria, refer to the Executive arm of government as the "administration" of whoever is President, their current one being the Barack Obama administration. They do not call it "the government of Barack Obama" as we sometimes misguidedly do in Nigeria.

The political party whose candidate is President – in theory an independent candidate can be one – may not necessarily be the one that has a majority of seats in the Legislature. Such a circumstance would have made the concepts of "government" and "opposition" further unexplainable. Assuming, for instance, that General Muhammadu Buhari of the Congress for Political Change (CPC) were the winner of the presidential election of April 2011, would the Peoples Democratic Party (PDP) have been regarded as an opposition party in spite of its control of the majority of seats in the Senate and House of Representatives?The CPC,not least because of its comparatively inferior representation in the Legislature, would hardly have qualified to be called the ruling party

The point one is trying to make here is that all political parties with elected members in the legislature constitute the government. Such

117

political parties are best described as "rivals" for power rather than being opposing parties in the context of adversarial politics. In a more developed democratic culture there would be no need for the so-called Government of National Unity that we often assume should be in place before the Executive arm of government can function. The President-elect should have had the confidence or given a free-hand to appoint his own team of ministers and advisers with the diversity of our nation in his or her mind. The role of the political party as an agent of integration, rather than that of sharing loots, would be more appreciated when we have had competitive political parties that traverse regional divides. The essence of this essay is to re-state a constitutional design which could make such a development feasible in the very near future.

Regardless of our legendary dishonesty, the idea of "zoning" or "rotation" has been, for decades, an integral part of our political discussions and calculations. However, its positive implications for integration have not been fully digested. Most tend to look at it from the pedestrian level of sharing political offices but it is more than that. This writer has clung to the idea of a formalised zoning arrangement, particularly at the level of the presidency, not least because of its positive implications for the electoral behaviour of Nigerians and the development of the party system generally.

It is illustrated in my publication, *The Search for a Nigerian Political System* (1986) that a deliberate policy of choosing presidential contestants from a particular region or ethno-sectional constituency would produce two possible outcomes, each complimenting the other.

The first of such outcomes is the weakening of the bastion of ethnicity because of the intra-ethnic competition that has been introduced. The second outcome would be how the fact of the absence of an "ethnic" candidate in an election has reflected on voting behaviour in the national constituency. Voters are likely to be more objective and rational in making electoral choices than they would otherwise have been. The 2011 presidential election, if one must be honest, has been one in which divisive sentiments came to the fore.

In the 1999 presidential election when the choice was between Chief Olu Falae and General Olusegun Obasanjo, both Yoruba, there were those of us who assumed, for instance, that the latter might be more experienced in handling the issue of military involvement in politics. The military had constituted itself into a political nuissance and it was always assumed it would intervene in politics for selfish reasons. Of course there were also those who thought Falae might be a better manager of the economy. Chief Falae had previously been Minister of Finance and was not indicted of corruption, making such an assumption reasonable. There was, in short, some kind of rational thinking here that would hardly have been contemplated in a clash involving ethnic candidates.

Had we continued with that electoral approach, we would by now have had manageable political parties that traverse the divides. There would have been no place for the mushroom political parties whose leaders end up endorsing the candidates of other political parties! The so-called progressive political parties, previously constrained by the ethnic factor, would have had little or no problem in coalescing into a broad-based political party. Our choices at election time might have been better clarified, while the prospect of conducting a free and fair election might also have been better helped.

The Goodluck Jonathan administration is enjoined to make a review of the Constitution one of its priorities. It is suggested that this be embarked upon very early in its life in order to ensure its thoroughness and completion. We would need to transform our nation into a functioning federation as well as anchor our democracy on the rotation of leadership. The position one is re-stating here is that a nation of wise men and women can decide its own structure of democracy based on its historical experiences and peculiarities. It serves no useful purpose being myopically preoccupied with the political arrangements of nations whose origins and complexities differ from ours.

*The Guardian, 23 May 2011*

# For the Democracy of Individual Choice

The "glory days" of Nigerian democratic politics were in the 1950s when electioneering periods were like festive occasions for us young children. The rare opportunity to see the Awos, the Ziks and the Sardaunas was anticipated with feverish anxiety, the type of anxiety with which we awaited great festive occasions.

I witnessed two exciting elections in the late 1950s – the 1957 election to the Western House of Assembly and the 1959 federal election – before the game of democratic politics succumbed to the "hoodlum culture". The old Western Region which is the focus of this article, hosted two historic political parties – the Action Group (AG) led by Chief Obafemi Awolowo and the National Council of Nigeria and the Cameroons (as it then was), led by Dr Nnamdi Azikiwe. The then Western Region was warmly described by eminent political scholars as one example of an emerging two-party state.

The region, comprised mainly of the Yoruba, could hardly have been a one-party state. A history of inter-tribal wars meant it was porous, as intra-communal conflicts arising from depositions and chieftaincy tussles also fuelled divisions. Additionally, a history of violent disputations over territorial boundaries meant one community was likely to shun a political party that had been widely embraced by another. There was very little space for ideology in the exciting politics of this era.

Nevertheless, there is still a sense on which it can be argued that the keen competition between the NCNC and the AG contributed immensely to the great achievements we have continued to credit to the immortal Chief Obafemi Awolowo, first Premier of the Western Region. He was, perhaps, the only one of the "triumvirates", which included Sir Ahmadu Bello of the Northern Region and Dr Nnamdi Azikiwe of the Eastern Region, who had to ensure a most critical challenge from an opposition party. The city of Ibadan, seat of regional government, was dominated by the opposition party, the

NCNC. In fact, the NCNC won more seats than the ruling AG from the region's federal election of 1954. Chief Awolowo, however, thrived in the knowledge that the only way he could sustain his leadership as well as his party's rule was by wooing the electorate in achievable programmes such as the widely-acclaimed free education at the primary school level. He was a man of exceptional self-discipline, both in private as well as in public life.

Be that as it may, the Yoruba section of Nigerian society, otherwise known today as the South West, enjoyed a stint of one-party dominance during the Second Republic (1979-83) when the Unity Party of Nigeria (UPN) predominated in the Yoruba states. The UPN, led by Chief Obafemi Awolowo, was a re-incarnation of the Action Group. That unprecedented one-party dominance came as a result of the crisis the Yoruba endured in the latter part of the First Republic. The intra-Action Group crisis of 1962 and the violence occasioned by the disputed regional election of 1965 were rightly or wrongly interpreted as the exploitation of Yoruba disunity by "external" influences. However, the UPN dominance had begun to weaken by the end of the Second Republic.

The current Republic (is it Third or Fourth?) began in 1999 with another recrudescence of AG/UPN – the Alliance for Democracy (AD) – holding sway in the South West. There was this appearance of a one-party dominated region until 2003 when President Olusegun Obasanjo desperately needed his ethnic kinsmen and women to support his re-election as President of the Federal Republic of Nigeria. General Obasanjo had won the presidential election of 1999 without meaningful support from the Yoruba. However, he successfully persuaded governors elected on the platform of AD to support his re-election and that support would prove to be their undoing, as Obasanjo's Peoples Democratic Party (PDP) "took over" the South West. That incursion might, however, prove to have been short-lived as the South West is now controlled by the Action Congress of Nigeria (ACN) – a somewhat recrudescence of AG/UPN/AD. The only Yoruba state outside the orbit of the ACN is Ondo where Labour is the governing party.

121

In spite of the seeming dominance of the ACN, the South West is reasonably competitive. The PDP presents viable opposition in most of the states and qualifies to be called the "alternative party". This rivalry or competition should be sustained because true democracy is about a people making a choice between alternatives. Even when there is a need for integration of some sort, the opportunity to be able to make a choice between alternatives remains that inalienable aspect of true democracy that cannot be taken away from the individual. Those who would want to assert their rule would have to learn a few lessons from the great Obafemi Awolowo's outstanding leadership.

For the simple reason that true democracy can only be nurtured and sustained by men and women of decent culture and morality, I dedicate this article to Chief Joel Babatola, the Olora of Ado-Ekiti, who exhibited these traits and impressed this writer so much in the early days. A gentleman, politician and minister of various ministries under the premierships of Chiefs Obafemi Awolowo and Samuel Ladoke Akinola, Chief J E Babatola cultivated friendship beyond the party divide. He was the quintessential practitioner of "politics without bitterness". The great Chief Babatola celebrated his 93rd birthday recently; long may he live!

*Daily Trust, 16 March 2012*

# Election rigging : When will it end?

Those wizards of Nollywood should now help us to laugh at our past by making a film on how elections have been lost and won in Nigeria. There was once a time when an opposition politician could wake up in the morning only to find a dead body deposited in his backyard! The alternative to being charged with murder and possibly facing the gallows would have been to switch political party allegiance without much persuasion.

Political intimidation and politics of thuggery were once like bread and butter. The politicians of old that were considered to be very powerful had those thugs who were prepared to kill or be killed on their behalf. Election rigging was not the sophisticated intervention it now has become but political thugs did play their own part. Sometime in the late 1950s an opposition politician in my constituency was very close to celebrating a rare electoral victory when suddenly the tears were forced from his eyes. As his victory was about to be concluded with not too many ballot boxes left to be counted, political thugs rushed into the hall and shuffled uncounted ballot papers with those already counted. A bye election was consequently arranged for the constituency but the ruling party had done its rigging homework to prevent a possible "upset". That episode, I must confess, revealed to me very early in life that elections in Nigeria were neither free nor fair.

In one particular region of the Nigerian federation we were told how overzealous party officials were able more or less to observe voters as they cast their votes. The officials would sit on raised platforms and monitor the direction in which prospective voters moved. If one was observed moving in the direction in which the ballot box belonging to an opposition party was situated, there would be an explanation to be made. It would have suggested to the officials that one did not vote for the party in power and punitive measures could be meted out.

Election rigging took a new dimension once Nigeria became independent in 1960. Ballot boxes were often stuffed with prestamped ballot papers. There were cases of women who appeared pregnant while going into the polling booths, having padded their tummies with ballot papers, only to re-emerge with their "babies" already delivered! In the old Western Region the leadership of the ruling Nigerian National Democratic Party (NNDP) made voting almost irrelevant as electoral officials, on their behalf, declared rival politicians as having accepted defeat voluntarily by withdrawing from pre-arranged contests.

The current culture of "awarding" votes and seats to competing political parties became an additional innovation in 1983 when the ruling National Party of Nigeria (NPN) imposed its candidates on constituencies where the party's support base suggested otherwise. Twenty years later in 2003 the same rigging approach was witnessed by international observers who wrote honest reports about the shame of our nation. They reported on how recorded votes far outnumbered the names on registered voters' lists and how the police, in their usual custom, became accomplices in the rigging exercise. Rigging has become something we have all come to expect as unavoidable in every election and the putative 2007 one is already blemished as an election that has already been rigged – an assumption that can hardly be refuted, with the discovery of voting machines in private homes.

The consequences of election rigging have been grave. It should be recollected that violent protests over the rigged 1965 Western regional elections hastened the first military intervention in Nigerian politics. Similarly, in 1983, violent protests over the NPN's incursion into "unfriendly" constituencies contributed in no small measure to the collapse of the Second Republic. If history is not to repeat itself, the forthcoming "transition" election must be approached with exceptional caution.

The stakes are high in 2007, and an atmosphere of bitterness already permeates the national environment. President Olusegun Obasanjo sees the 2007 presidential election as a "do or die" battle, not least because of his perception of it as a verdict on his own legacy. Vice President Atiku Abubakar, who has pitched his political tent with the

Action Congress (AC) parades his part in the proposed contest as a show of strength between himself and his boss. An influential foreign magazine already assumes that political exile could be the best option for Obasanjo were his feuding deputy to be the next president. General Muhammadu Buhari of the All Nigerian Peoples Party (ANPP), on his part, believes the yet-to-take-place election has already been concluded in favour of the ruling party. He believed, rightly or wrongly, that he was cheated in 2003.

With so much at stake, and with so much bitterness around, a bitterly contested presidential election could claim a few casualties. The "speed boat" which Dr Reuben Abati talked about in a recent entertaining article could, in fact, be around the corner for the privileged few who might want to get out of trouble quickly. One has heard Nigerians living abroad warn friends to wait until after the elections before visiting Nigeria. What an irony!

Politics in Nigeria is big business. It confers instant prominence on quite a number of people who have little talent for other things. Those who today are at the helm of national affairs cannot contemplate life on the other side of the political fence. In some societies those who have lost out in the political game have other attractive options to fall back on but this is hardly so in the Nigerian society of today. The rigging culture is likely to continue to embarrass our nation and frustrate its development until politics becomes the game for those who have no cause to see it as a "do or die" battle. However, the process of taming an unenviable monster would have been set in motion if President Olusegun Obasanjo could view the pending 2007 election as an integral part of his own political legacy, regardless of who the next president of the Nigerian federation is.

*The Guardian,13 March 2007*

# Parties and Elections, the British Example

Nigeria's ruling People's Democratic Party (PDP) might have conceived or contrived an idea of remaining in power for the next 50 years but such an assumption of unmerited longevity would seem rather laughable in real democratic nations of the world as their politicians hardly look beyond one election at a time. The retention of political power is not about being a member of the political party in power, it is about how the people perceive their individual and collective well-being over a period of time. They would ask those seeking their votes, especially the political party in power, "are we better off today than we were when we voted you into power four or five years ago?" If the majority conclude that their lot did not improve, it would have to be goodbye to those they hold responsible for their plight, also the time for change would have come. It is all about people power.

However, the alternative they seek must be credible. Those seeking to unseat others must be able to convince the electorate that the change they promise to make is real. The choice the people have to make becomes clarified when they are in a position to know, for instance, where one political party is different from the other. Mere sloganeering will not do. The British political parties are ideological and issue-oriented parties and their approaches to the organisation of state and society have people in no doubt as what to expect whenever one of the major ones, Labour or Conservative, is in power.

The dominant issues in Britain's recent election, not necessarily in their order of importance, include the economy, immigration and electoral reform. Just coming out of a recession, the sustenance of the economy assumed its indispensable priority in the campaigns, cutting the deficit and amending the weaknesses in the current monetary policy. People are worried about their jobs, taxes, mortgages and other mundane aspects of human existence, which include health and security. Of equal importance in the campaign is the issue of immigration. Not many Britons are comfortable with the influx of foreigners into their country. Membership of the European Union has undoubtedly led to the influx of people from the former Eastern Bloc. The Labour Party would argue that Britain has benefited substantially from the presence of immigrants but such a view is not shared by the Conservative Party which is less favourably disposed towards Europe. The promise of the Liberal Democrats to grant amnesty to illegal immigrants might not have been music to many ears.

The 2010 British election has proved to be one of the most exciting and keenly contested in recent decades, resulting in a hung parliament. The Conservative Party won the largest number of seats, followed by Labour and the Liberal Democrats in a distant third. The constitution however empowers a sitting Prime Minister to try and form a government in the circumstances, an opportunity that the Labour Party might want to exploit by striking a deal with the Liberal Democrats. The next British government, whether led by Labour or the Conservatives, will be a coalition one with all its implications.

What should however be of great interest to us in Nigeria is that the issue of electoral reform is still dominant in this ancient and accomplished democratic nation. The leadership of the Liberal Democrats wants a reform of the voting system; they prefer proportional representation (PR) to the single-member, first-past-the-post system that is much favoured by Labour and the Conservatives. Their argument is that proportional representation would better reflect in parliament the support the political parties enjoy nationally. The danger with proportional representation is that the House of Commons could be 'crowded' with representatives of mushroom political parties and this may not augur well for decision-making and policy formulation, as well as for the apportionment of credit or blame in those respects. Neither Labour nor the Conservatives want proportional representation. There can never be an end to reforms and new ideas in the democratic process.

Although Great Britain may have been the coloniser of many nations of the world, its politicians are still learning from others. American-style presidential debates are the main features of electioneering in Britain in 2010, almost 50 years after America's first televised debates between John Kennedy and Richard Nixon in 1960. Even when the

British Prime Minister is not elected nationally- people vote for their local representatives- the debates help substantially in educating people about the positions of the political parties on major issues, as well as the preparedness and style of their political leaders. Debates between political protagonists are undoubtedly recommended to societies where people are educated and rational enough to benefit from the choices with which they are presented.

The manner in which the British elections are conducted is also something to be admired. The campaign lasted barely four weeks and not a single related death was reported. There were no fraudulent issues with ballot papers, or the outcome of the elections. Voters' registration cards came through the post, as the ages and addresses of every person resident in Britain are available in the records. Pensioners could be seen as volunteers, helping prospective voters at the polling stations. Neither was election day a public holiday; people enthusiastically exercised their mandates during their free time. We in Nigeria have a lot to learn from the British approach to democracy.

We must learn, as a matter of urgency, that democracy is not a matter of 'do or die'. Elections must be free and fair, and a people represented by those they have duly chosen. It cannot but be emphasised here that one admirable beauty of contemporary British electoral process is that there were neither police officers nor armed soldiers at the polling stations, neither were there party officials to monitor voting. It was taken for granted that people would conduct themselves in orderly and civilised manners. Minor flaws in the British elections, which include shortage of ballot papers in a few polling stations, and the fact that a few hundred could not vote because the law mandated elections to end by 10 pm, were promptly acknowledged by the Independent Electoral Commission. Democracy should not be about the 'ambition' of individuals but the future of society. The political party of the future needs a leadership and following that are committed to the vision of society they seek for themselves and their children's children.

*The Guardian 10 May 2010*

# PART 6

# THE MONSTER OF CORRUPTION

## SYNOPSIS

*Perhaps the most important and very urgent challenge today is how to end the culture of graft and corruption in the Nigerian society. Nigeria is a relatively rich nation, blessed with agricultural and mineral resources - a major oil producing nation of the world. However, corruption has impeded progress in an otherwise dynamic nation. Corruption eats deep into the fabrics of society but politicians are the worst for it. The Nigerian politician is like the armed robber, determined to cart away whatever they can lay their hands upon. The Olusegun Obasanjo administration, 1999-2007, established the Economic and Financial Crimes Commission, EFCC, to fight official corruption, but it would appear that corruption is one fight for the generality of Nigerians.*

## A History of Corruption

Until President Obasanjo began his crusade against corruption via the Anti-Corruption law, "Welcome to the country of corruption" would have been an appropriate inscription at Nigeria's international airports! The anxiety of airport officials to extort money from those travelling into and out of the country, be they Nigerians or foreigners, was there for all to see. To the corrupt members of the police force, any criminal was welcome provided he paid the price being asked by the officer. And in the civil service, right from the messenger to the official at the very top, any duty performed was based on what could be extracted from whoever sought their services. In short, corruption pervaded every stratum of Nigerian society. The use of the past tense is not to suggest that Nigeria has now been transformed into a corruption free environment.

Ranging from petty bribery to virtually ordering the Central Bank of Nigeria to siphon money into private bank accounts in overseas countries, corruption takes various forms that only a specialist in the subject will be keen to detail. The usual defence of the small offender is to blame corruption on the extended family system, which puts heavy demands on meagre earnings, but when it comes to the scale of graft by those at the top echelons of government it is nothing but greed. The only reason why Nigeria is underdeveloped and indebted to the IMF is the corruption of the trustees of the national purse. Such corruption has tended to be on the increase with successive governments since independence in 1960.

The prominent politicians of the First Republic (1960-1966) were flamboyant, rode in Pontiacs and Chevrolets, and lived in big houses. Although corruption was not an issue, as regional rivalry and inter-party wrangling were the dominant themes during this era, Major Chukwuma Kaduna Nzeogwu, the man who directed their overthrow, nevertheless described them as "ten-percenters", i.e., they demanded ten per cent of the value of contracts they awarded. In fact many politicians, both at the regional and federal levels of government, were indicted by the military administration that eventually took over the reins of government.

The succeeding government headed by Major General J.T.U. Aguiyi-Ironsi could be said to have consisted of true professionals who were more accustomed to life in the officers' mess than the luxury of the outside. Many of the top officers never built houses of their own and were not "permitted" to stay long in office to be tainted with accusations of corruption.

The same could hardly be said of the soldiers who overthrew the Ironsi administration. The civil war (1967-70) and the oil wealth during the Gowon era (July 1966-July 1975) brought a new dimension to official corruption in Nigeria. It was an era of "boom" for soldiers and their surrogates who masqueraded as contractors. While General Yakubu Gowon himself has continued to live a relatively modest life style since being ousted from power (he is said not to have built a house for himself while in office), ten of his twelve state governors were indicted for corruption and self-enrichment by the Murtala Muhammed-Obasanjo administration.

The Murtala-Obasanjo government (1975-79) deserved to be described as a "corrective" regime as it made frantic efforts to sanitise society by its purge of officials who were either corrupt or unproductive, and its strict adherence to policies and programmes outlined for a return to civilian rule. However, that administration could not be said to be free of corruption accusations or insinuations. Certain individuals were believed to have been enriched through money paid for contracts that were partly performed or not performed at all. Some principal members of the government retired to embark on business ventures that could back up the suggestion that they had used their positions to enrich themselves while in office. For instance, the late Major-General Shehu Musa Yar'Adua emerged from government to become a bank owner and one of the richest Nigerians of his time. Lt.-General Theophilus Danjuma is a wealthy individual, while General Olusegun Obasanjo's farm at Ota has been described as a village of its own. The late Chief Awolowo referred to Obasanjo's farm as a "latifundia" in a bitter letter he wrote to the latter which was published by the Nigerian Tribune in December 1979, and it cannot be forgotten that the late Fela Anikulapo Kuti made scurrilous references to the general in the International Thief Thief (ITT) record.

Be that as it may, Obasanjo faithfully handed over power to an elected government and that stood him in good stead. But the return of democracy in the Shehu Shagari era (1979-83) meant the return of the political termites and the democratisation of corruption. Corruption was witnessed in every level of government, and was not limited to any political party. However, the NPN-controlled executive was the worst offender. The competition by NPN stalwarts to own private jets and outsmart one another in the amount of money stashed in overseas banks was unprecedented. Most Nigerians hailed the overthrow of the politicians of the Second Republic. Their excesses were such that the late Chief J.M. Johnson, a prominent politician in the First Republic, prayed never again to witness democracy in his lifetime.

Senator Arthur Nzeribe, himself a member of the legislature, organised a rally in London in support of the soldiers who had overthrown a civilian government he described as very corrupt. Many of the politicians were consigned into detention by the Buhari-Idiagbon government, and large sums of money recovered from them. An attempt was made to "crate" Umaru Dikko from the United Kingdom to Nigeria to face charges of corruption, of which he was the acknowledged czar.

The incoming administration of Major-General Muhammadu Buhari (1984-85) and his new conquerors of democracy is better remembered for its tyranny and "triple standard" in political decisions than for corruption, although it must be said that the prominent actors some of whom had served under the Murtala-Obasanjo administration, refused to declare their assets publicly on assumption of office. What the era gave to the world of corruption was General Ibrahim Babangida who overthrew his colleagues in a palace coup, and established a government of his own.

The Babangida government (1985-93), it must be emphasised, elevated corruption to an instrument of state policy. General Babangida would seem to have believed that every Nigerian had a price tag on his head. This was described by General Obasanjo as a policy of "settling" opponents. The government enriched its actors and many friends, and General Babangida himself is not doing badly in the life of unexplainable luxury into which he was forced to retire. The culmination of corruption and robbery during the Babangida era was the case of the nation's windfall from oil during the Gulf crisis - a windfall estimated at about $12 billion - which is yet to be accounted for.

Babangida was the decent operator compared with General Sani Abacha (1993-98) who transformed Nigeria into a family company in which every member was a shareholder. The Governor of the Central Bank of Nigeria was accountable to the family, and had to make available whatever sums of money were demanded by any of its members. Revelations have continued to be made of Abacha's billions in foreign bank accounts, and the wealth of his collaborators is known to many Nigerians.

The sudden death of Abacha is a classic moral lesson about vanity. However, his successor, General Abdusalami Abubakar, would appear to have ignored this lesson. He satisfied his own urge and those of his close associates by dipping both hands into the national pie before leaving office. The Christopher Kolade inquiry set up by President Obasanjo indicted the Abubakar administration in its findings over contract awards and financial transactions that were hastily made between June 1998 and May 1999.

The entry of the civilian politicians, with President Obasanjo's emphasis on the eradication of corruption, brought succour to an embattled citizenry who had witnessed the worst excesses of authoritarian rule. Elected politicians, unlike military dictators, are accountable to the Nigerian electorate, and that is why democracy must be protected at all costs. The revelations of corruption in the Senate, which resulted in the impeachment of its president (Dr Chuba Okadigbo) and the resignation of top officers, are sad but encouraging in the sense that the Idris Kuta probe was instituted by the senators themselves. The crusade against corruption at the governmental level must be a continuous process. The crusade has not ceased in Great Britain, one of the oldest democracies of the world. What is significant in Britain is that a case of corruption, once identified, does not go unpunished. The House of Commons continues to reform itself, as evidenced by the rule requiring every member to enter into the register of interests any commitment outside Parliament, even the publication of an article in a newspaper, which brings in a financial reward of more than £500.

To fight corruption in society at large, successive governments must identify policies that seek to eradicate ignorance and poverty. The way to eradicate ignorance is for governments to invest in a system of education which, from primary to university level, teaches the citizenry about their civic and legal rights among other things. As for poverty, governments must provide opportunities for the people and social security for those who are unemployed or unemployable. The crusade against poverty must include improvements in transport, housing and health facilities, so that those on minimum earnings can still live with contentment.

Attempt to give a gift of money to a British youngster, and the ninety per cent probability is that he or she will ask you, "What for"? One can hardly say that about the Nigerian counterpart, and that is why poverty is the very root cause of corruption in society.

*June 2002*

# The iniquity of greed

I once talked about the "iniquity of greed" with a Nigerian I met in London sometime in the 1980s. The meeting place was at the then African Concord House, owned by the late Chief MKO Abiola, where I had more or less established a perennial presence not least to read Nigerian newspapers. Those of the internet age might wonder why one would have had to travel all the way from Oxford to London for the purpose of reading newspapers; the internet generation does not have to "travel" out of their bedrooms in order to read anything but this was not the case in the 1980s. Nigerian newspapers were flown to Britain and other parts of the world by various agents.

Be that as it may, I met this Nigerian in London and for some strange reason we did not introduce ourselves. Maybe the reason I did not introduce myself - even when not quite used to frivolous introductions -was because of what happened at African 'Concord House. As we scrambled for the newspapers, some as old as weeks, this fellow grabbed one which had published an article of mine. He seemed to be excited by it as he yelled, "yes, it is Anthony Akinola again. His articles stand out among those of other Nigerians. He is always writing about structures that can move Nigeria forward. I think he is looking for political appointment".

Naturally I felt pleased by what he had to say about Anthony Akinola and I did not hesitate to say, "you can never tell with these writers". A member of staff of the African Concord magazine glanced at me, marvelling at the fact that someone could be talking about the very person standing next to them without knowing it. The article which sparked his comments was one I had written, furthering my arguments about the desirability of a rotational presidency in Nigeria.

It is not always true that one would be writing solely for selfish reasons. Without the passion for writing, one can hardly achieve longevity as a writer. Of course a writer may get noticed and invited to play a role where his or her expertise is relevant but this would not mean they deliberately courted it. Maybe we should not impute motives into what others do.

Now to this important matter of the iniquity of greed, the discussion was provoked by our reflection on the fall of the Second Republic (1979-1983). One epitaph of that era was provided by General Olusegun Obasanjo who castigated the government of the Second Republic for having spent over 50 billion naira - a colossal sum in those days - in less than four years with nothing to show for it. The military regime led by General Obasanjo, had voluntarily handed over power to a civilian administration led by Alhaji Shehu Shagari in October 1979; that voluntary transfer of political power from one government to another, a hitherto unprecedented feat on the African continent, enhanced the dignity of General Obasanjo considerably in the eyes of the world and must have given him some kind of moral authority to indulge in lecturing others about how a government should be run. However, his critics might not concede he still has that moral authority today, having himself presided over a somewhat prodigal civilian administration between 1999 and 2007.

With the possible exception of a tiny minority of its members, the politicians of the Second Republic were a despicable horde. In spite of the poor state our universities were and still are in, there were quite a number of them donating monies to educational institutions of rich nations in return for lousy, honorary degrees. I wrote angrily about this when I was studying in the United States. Not just a few of the Second Republic politicians had private jets, while rabbits compete with dangerous vehicles for the right of way in our so-called public roads. Our hospitals, as rightly described by their equally incompetent military conquerors, were no better than "mere consulting clinics". When the fall of the Second Republic came, it was an occasion of great joy to impoverished Nigerians.

The politicians of today are hardly any different from their disgraced predecessors. Many will say they are even worse! Their intention to defraud the public becomes evident in the dubious assets most of them declare. A hitherto unemployed university graduate would have no qualms about declaring an asset worth tens of millions of naira, all in anticipation of what could be stolen while in office. Assets declared by politicians are accepted in good faith, their authenticity never verified or established.

Many Nigerians would want to go into politics today, not because they want to serve their nation but because they want to be rich. The salaries and allowances our elected politicians corner to themselves would amaze their counterparts even in the truly rich nations of the world. A senator of the Federal Republic of Nigeria earns more money than the President of the United States of America. The Nigerian politician wins regular lottery in corrupt practices or shady deals. The saving grace for democracy of today, if one must be honest, has been the distrust Nigerians have for the military. The experiences of governance between 1985 and 1998 do not recommend further military involvement in politics.

Nigerians now call for a revolution, which is to say that there can be no peace when the majority of our peoples live in abject poverty, while a tiny minority lives in gluttonous greed. The majority of our people love democracy and are peace-loving; however, disruptive tendencies can find easy recruitment in the ranks of the uneducated and the impoverished. It is both in the short-term and long-term interest of our nation that we enrich our peoples educationally and economically. To be able to do this, we must put an end to corruption and greed.

*Daily Trust, 22 July 2011*

# Defrauding the public

Not necessarily because they hate other nations but principally because of their own perennial inadequacies, pseudo-democrats of the African continent tend to enjoy it when some calamity is befalling democracy in one of its celebrated domains. When, in the year 2000, disputed elections in the State of Florida badly smeared the American presidential election there were not just a few "outsiders" who gleefully mocked the process. Mr. Robert Mugabe of Zimbabwe laughed loud about it and would have even been laughing much louder now that a scandal of historic proportion is rocking the British Parliament, his erstwhile nemesis, over the expenses of its members. "These things do happen everywhere" has become a trademark commiseration for our collective failings as a people.

Of course things do happen everywhere but the question remains as to who is actually learning from its mistakes and who seems to be perpetuating theirs. The Florida episode of 2000 became the global story that it was because what we saw fell short of what we had come to expect of the United States of America as a leading democratic nation. However, the almost hitch-free subsequent elections (2004 and 2008) more or less highlight Florida 2000 as an exception rather than the rule. Compare and contrast this with the democratic history of the Federal Republic of Nigeria, for instance. Is there any electoral issue, election rigging for instance, which brought down its previous republics in 1966 and 1983 that can be said today to have been a mere historical event?

The honest answer to this rather rhetorical question would be "none", not least because election rigging is as celebrated in Nigeria today as it was in the 1960s when politicians boasted openly that the people's votes meant nothing to them. However, this is not an open invitation for the over-ambitious soldier to start planning a speech! Maybe we would have learnt some lessons, painful but beneficial, if coupists had not taken advantage of the situations we found ourselves in, in the past. Their coups might have been popular at the times they took place but they would now appear to have added little or no value to our Nigerian society. The coupists spoke voluminously about corruption in society but their speeches are today mere metaphors in irony.

Nigeria's corrupt politicians of today would have attempted to play down their own greed with events in Britain where many members of parliament have been indicted of falsifying their expenses. The bad news for them, however, is that those British "fraudsters" cannot get away with it as they do in Nigeria. Some of them have been sacked from their privileged positions and most if not all know that they are spending their last days as representatives of the British people as they would be deselected from future elections. The Speaker of the House, Mr. Michael Martin, has been forced to tender his resignation; he is the first Speaker of the House to face such ignominy since 1695. The police, of course, have been busy with investigations that could lead to criminal prosecution of "dishonourable" men and women and the jails could soon be welcoming them. The privilege of "self regulation" which goes with the sovereignty of parliament could be ceded to an independent statutory body which would determine the expenses of the law-makers.

In contrast to the culture of impunity that pervades our leadership, Prime Minister Gordon Brown wrote to every British household "I know that people are angry about MPs' expenses, I apologise - on behalf of all parties - that the political system has let you and the public down. Whatever party they belong to, MPs should never have spent taxpayers' money on clearing their moats or swimming pools, or paying phantom mortgages - and it's even worse at a time when ordinary families are worried about the impact of the recession..."

The British people are indeed angry at the misdemeanour of their electoral representatives and there should be no mistake about this. Many donors have withdrawn their financial support to the ruling Labour Party and the pendulum of power could be swinging elsewhere come general elections. The British economy is tax-based; the British people genuinely feel aggrieved that it is their money that some privileged individuals have been stealing. Maybe we in Nigeria do not always feel their type of anger, not least because of the assumption that money stolen by our own politicians is some kind of "windfall" from oil. Maybe we should start paying taxes as a way of fortifying our authority over our collective wealth and making sure that those we put in charge of our nation's tills are accountable.

The democratic journey is indeed an eternal one, a journey that continues for as long as the nation itself lives. The more enlightened a people are the better for democracy and the good things that come along with it. Is it not true that those of us whose lives have been made awkward by the corruption of politicians are the very ones who encourage the triumph of this monster in our society? The political office holder is perceived as the lucky one, the one who must make full use of the opportunity before him or her. If the political office holder has not demonstrated wealth within a short period of time, his or her people would assume that an opportunity is being mis-used. Nigerians could be political, not least because they are most vociferous about elections.

There are many among them who could put their own lives on the line because of the ambition of a politician; however, once the politician is elected or selected into office, they cannot be bothered about how the enormous powers at his or her disposal are exercised. Members of the various constituencies hardly make any impact on the decisions that govern their own lives and neither do they get any feedback from their elected representatives who claim so much salary and expenses for constituency representation. Our lots will not improve if we fold our arms and await miracle to happen. We should, as urged by Tajudeen Abdul-Raheem of blessed memory, "organise, not agonise".

We must organise, not just against corruption and electoral malpractices, against politicians taking advantage of us in other respects. Frivolous trips to overseas countries, simply because they provide opportunities for some smart money to be made, defraud the common purse. The proposed course at Harvard, assumed to train our already elected governors on how to govern, is both laughable and disgraceful. The Guardian competently advised against this ridiculous proposal in its editorial of June 11, 2009, and all one is urging here is for their various constituencies to prevail against it.

*The Guardian, 15 June 2009*

## Somehow, Atiku could be right

A GOAT does not bite; however, there is this saying by the Yoruba that a goat can bite if driven against the wall. Of course every statement should be interpreted in the context in which it is made, but there is nothing really wrong in warning a people about an impending danger. It is a classic statement, applicable in all spheres of human endeavour, that 'those who make peaceful change impossible, make violent change inevitable'

Alhaji Atiku Abubakar, erstwhile Vice-President and now presidential aspirant under the platform of the ruling People's Democratic Party (PDP) might have warned of a possible violence in a rather selfish context as his critics would insist he did, that warning itself should however be heeded in the context of our failings since independence in 1960. Our nation is rotten, prompting the well-cultured and much-respected Professor Ben Nwabueze to advocate, rather out of character, a bloody revolution as panacea to the ills we celebrate in Nigeria.

Let us, for instance, take the conduct of our elections as one example. The failure to make a peaceful change possible via electoral outcome led to the violent overthrow, by coupists, of the First Republic on January 15, 1966. The politics of the First Republic was characterised by election rigging, both at regional and federal levels, of which that of the defunct Western Region in 1965 was the most blatant display of contempt for the feelings and aspirations of ordinary Nigerians by their so-called politicians. The fall of the Second Republic in 1983, on similar grounds, merely confirmed we are a people who hardly learn from history. Thankfully the courts now intervene to redress cases of electoral fraud, but for how long must we continue to flaunt our crudity before the rest of the world? Must the responsibility to determine who has won and who has not won an election now be ceded to the judicial arm of government?

We have elections slated for April 2011, but the fears we have always had about elections persist. Fear about political murders and assassinations is further exacerbated by a more devastating new culture of bomb blasts. The ranks and files of political thugs now have unemployed university graduates as recruits. The act of election rigging is being perfected on a daily basis, as confirmed by the recent theft of Direct Data Capturing Machines from an aircraft at the Murtala Muhammed International Airport. It is doubtful if such a theft could have been committed without the knowledge of powerful but dishonest politicians and the complicity of airport officials; the latter, corrupt as they ever are, can be trusted to agree to anything that has monetary reward.

Corruption itself is one culture that could soon compel violence in the Nigerian polity. Nigeria ranks among the most corrupt nations of the world, often alternating between first and second. Political office holders enrich themselves at the expense of taxpayers, in a society where most worship wealth rather than be bothered by its source. Any foreigner coming into Nigeria for the first time would know from our international airports that he or she is visiting a corrupt nation One recently visited Nigeria having travelled via Heathrow in Britain and De Gaulle Airport in France, but it was at the Murtala Muhammed International Airport that one got reminded of how crude human beings can be. Officials in uniform openly demand bribes and disgracefully beg for gifts. Every Nigerian including President Goodluck Jonathan knows that their nation is shamed right from its entry point.

What about our law-makers cornering about 25 per-cent of our national income to themselves? Dr. Lamido Sanusi, Governor of the Central Bank openly confronted these privileged Nigerians about their greed and profligacy to the delight of the rest of us. The greedy law-makers did not like his audacity but his was one kind of audacity of hope we so much cherish. Nigeria has earned so much from crude oil but with nothing to show for it in terms of development. The roads are bad; the hospitals are mere consulting clinics; our educational system is in consistent decline, the supply of electricity is epileptic, while that of water is equally unreliable in a nation that has most part of it in the rain forest.

Ghana, one of our neighbouring countries, is doing quite well. It should be worrying to our politicians, particularly our key leaders, that many Nigerians attribute the success of Ghana to the bloody revolt of Jerry Rawlings. Many wish to see the blood of their oppressors flow in the streets, they like to see those responsible for their economic plight tied to the stakes and given the Rawlings treatment. It should be recalled that, on July 16, 1979, Flt-Lieutenant Jerry Rawlings ordered the execution, by firing squad, of three former Heads of State, along with five other senior military officers, for various offences which include corruption. We hardly need an Atiku to warn of the inevitability of such a violent intervention because our politicians have been deliberately calling for it through their actions and inactions.

Even if Atiku Abubakar was talking from a selfish point of view, do we have to experience another national crisis before resolving a critical problem of nationhood known to all of us? Our politicians are selfish, opportunistic and dishonest. The opportunities to redress the imbalance in our federation were wasted in the pursuit of selfish, short-term agenda. One recent example was the so-called constitutional conference sponsored by the administration of General Olusegun Obasanjo with the sole intention of ratifying a third-term agenda.

There was a popular clamour at that time for the principle of leadership rotation to be entrenched in the constitution, but a great opportunity was wasted. It should be recollected that every major crisis in our unique federation, since independence in 1960, has revolved around leadership and a more honest and pragmatic people would have since proffered a realistic solution to it. The saying that things can only get better after they have become worst could suggest there are some harsh lessons to be learnt.

*The Guardian, 29 December 2010*

# The Mad Pursuit of Power

One definition of "power" as a concept in political science is provided by Dimitri Kousoulas as "the ability to make others do what they would not normally do on their own accord". The doctor asks your wife to take off her top and he starts examining her breast before your naked eyes. You have no objections; indeed you are more than happy to be told that she doesn't have cancer. However, were you suddenly to find the same wife in a similar position with someone else you would probably do more damage to her or the "intruder" than Mike Tyson did to Evander Holyfield's ear before you recover your composure!

The armed robber also has power even though it is not one that is backed with authority. Fear for one's life makes one hand over possessions and do whatever the armed robber orders in the circumstances. However, the power the elected "man of power" enjoys dwarfs that of the doctor or the armed robber. In a crude democracy where the power of the executive includes that of dishonestly accumulating and dispensing wealth, the armed robber in particular envies the effortless grace with which that function is performed.

The brother of a friend of mine was "running mate" in a gubernatorial election and by virtue of his party winning that election he became Deputy Governor. Suddenly my telephone began to enlist some interesting conversations: "How is your friend the brother of the Deputy Governor?" "When is he going back to Nigeria?" "Now that his brother is Deputy Governor, don't you think he should be able to find something worthwhile doing in the state?

Of course my friend is one fiercely independent-minded individual who is well-acquainted with how power is sensibly exercised in Britain; he merely laughed off the new stardom his kinsmen were quick to impose on him. However, the unpaid-for political science lesson was not lost on him in that the Nigerian society itself puts untold pressure on the elected executive and more or less wills them into doing the evil things they are quite capable of doing.

The powers of the executive are clearly stated in the constitution and those powers are quite awesome. With immunity from prosecution while in office boldly inserted in the constitution, they are the type of powers that can be easily abused if they find their way into the open hands of a political miscreant. The dominant Nigerian subservient and sycophantic culture, un-helped by society poverty and mass illiteracy, provides no moral restraint or checks. Nigerian political culture expects the man of power to exercise power to the maximum and the philosophy of "if you cannot beat them, join them" offers little sympathy for dissent

A study in the psychology of why the average Nigerian wants to be president or governor should be interesting and revealing but one can make an educated guess here that the power and prestige the position confers would be right at the top. Such power and prestige, of course, include predominantly economic advantages. In some societies where the people are quite capable of linking their collective poverty to the corruption and greed of the political elite, and they resent it, the report that a former governor has 50 billion (fifty billion naira) in his bank account would probably have sent people rioting in the streets. In fact, a substantiated allegation of graft, embezzlement or corruption on the part of leadership would have meant that some political careers would come to an abrupt end.

The power of knowledge and ambition to redirect the course of a resentful history offers little appeal if not backed with economic power. When Chief Gani Fawehinmi offered himself as a presidential candidate in the 2003 election I knew he was one visionary who had no chance. Nigeria's politics of today is money politics as the poor look only for immediate, though temporary, salvation and not some promise of a better future for themselves and their children's children. Only the rich and powerful can offer the type of immediate salvation they seek and the Nigerian rich and powerful resent opposition or rivalry to their perceived entrenched positions. Hence the spate of killings and political assassinations since the inception of partisan politics in 1999.

Nigeria's politics will not change without a fundamental change in the current perceptions and attitudes of our people. Education should not be solely certificate-oriented but a veritable tool of assertiveness for individual rights and equality of men and women created by God. The leaders we have today believe they are there to be worshipped and when they squander public money they want to be thanked for their generosity. Their assumptions must be challenged by a generation of forward-looking Nigerians and a judiciary that stands for justice and not collusion.

There are some today who believe that politics is their family business, not least because they have no relevance outside it. To challenge them is to challenge their relevance and means of livelihood. They like it when the decent men of society conclude that politics is a dirty game because it means there is limited challenge to their trade. Maybe we must now change our perception of politics because although it may be a dirty game, it is that "dirty" that determines our present and our future. Politics is great if we can flush the dirty men out of it.

This article is dedicated to the memory of Dr. Ayo Daramola with whom I was somehow acquainted at Howard University in Washington DC. I had a feeling he would be involved in partisan politics; sadly, the veracity of that feeling was only confirmed to me by the shocking news of his violent extermination by those we suspect might have been his intolerant political opponents or rivals. He was an active participant in Howard student politics as well as that of Ekiti indigenes in the United State. A gentleman and scholar, may God rest his soul.

The spate of political assassinations should not provide the coward with justification for criminal silence in the struggle to move Nigeria forward. Anyone who has become jelly because of this political bullying, to the point of mortgaging his or her conscience, should not have been born in the first place. We shall all die at some stage and the manner of individual exit is a matter for destiny. Our collective preoccupation at the moment should be to fish out the cowards behind the murders of well-meaning Nigerians and bring such cowards to justice.

*The Guardian, 23 August 2006*

# Beyond mere grumbling

What has become rather customary whenever we commemorate our independence is for quite a number of writers to want to review the state of the nation. Expectedly, leadership is blamed for the litany of woes. While it can hardly be contradicted that leadership has failed in its responsibilities to Nigerians, the position one takes here is that we, the followers, have also failed ourselves in some respects. We have failed to check the greed and corruption of leadership, thereby contributing inadvertently to the abysmal failure to achieve the goals of development in our not-too-poor political entity.

There is this assumption that politicians have sacrificed their time and resources to get into public positions because of their patriotism. This may be true elsewhere but not in Nigeria. Most of those who hold public positions in our society today are where they are because of the alluring prospects of power, fame and fortune. . They would not be in politics if it were otherwise.

Be that as it may, our elected politicians nevertheless owe us a duty because they would not be where they are without our votes. They are our representatives; however, their failure is also an indictment of our ability to dictate the terms. We must accept that we have failed in this respect.

Political representation is a two-way process; there is an input and there is a feedback. The feedback generates further input. This, indeed, is how it works in a proper representative democracy. But how many of the so-called intelligentsia in our various communities can claim to have held meetings with their representatives regarding the plights and aspirations of their local constituencies? The representatives award themselves huge sums of money as constituency allowances but in what respects have these allowances been justified? Our young ladies are being sexually harassed here and there by prospective employers and those who should be in fiduciary positions but how many of our representatives have taken up their complaints

149

and work towards a law that makes sexual harassment a punishable offence?

The great Wole Soyinka was once optimistic that it would no longer be business as usual with our elected leaders. He indicated an intention to float a non-political interest group that would make its presence felt in the corridors of power nationwide. One hopes this inspirational genius of our generation would still be there to contribute to the founding of such a desirable association. An example of a non-partisan interest group in the USA is Common Cause whose activities have benefited ordinary Americans since it was founded in 1970.

We in Nigeria have been treated to how a non-partisan interest group can identify and stand up for what is good for all. The Save Nigeria Group, led by Pastor Tunde Bakare and others, proved that politicians can be forced to be responsible if those who elected them can also put some pressure on them. The Save Nigeria Group which sprung into action following the controversy generated by the incapacitation of the late President Umaru Musa Yar'adua should have transformed into a permanent interest group. It is sad that it did not.

There was always very little the "one-man bands" of the Tai Solarins and Gani Fawehinmis could have achieved. Dr Tajudeen Abdul-Raheem, the late Pan-Africanist campaigner and scholar, said we should "organise, not agonise". If we are genuinely concerned about our plights and rights, maybe it is time we organise ourselves into a non-partisan group, subscribed to by patriotic Nigerians across the various divides. The trouble with Nigeria is significantly that of a followership that would rather grumble than act collectively in pursuit of desired objectives.

We all accept that corruption is the cancer killing our nation but what have we done about it collectively? How many of us, including those who influence pubic opinion, can claim to be immune from it? How many of our professors or journalists would rather appear before the magistrate and be fined for committing a traffic offence than bribe the police?

Corruption will not go away unless we genuinely resent it and are prepared to vent our anger. There is one Anna Hazare, an Indian currently leading a campaign against corruption in his equally corrupt society: he has been able to inspire millions of his compatriots and the results are showing. The same can be done in Nigeria. It is a matter of a people taking a stand on what they claim they deplore. Our politicians can be cowed if we can insist we are no "idiots". Was it not the fear of Boko Haram and that of the Movement for the Emancipation of the Niger Delta (MEND) that forced our political leaders to abandon the traditional Eagle Square and celebrate independence anniversary in relative obscurity?

The message is simple: when we are no longer out there to marvel at the sight of palaces and obscenely expensive cars, proceeds of corruption that they are, our politicians will think twice about their greed-inspired indulgences and aspirations. We must deploy the power of education to free our peoples from the psychology of servitude imposed by some overbearing culture.

*Daily Trust, 10 October 2011*

# PART 7

# THE FALLACY OF WELFARISM

## SYNOPSIS

*The good intentions or pretentions of government regarding the welfare of the governed must be realistic, achievable as well as sustainable. These are areas of activities where the intervention of governments are both desirable and inevitable if society must progress and advance. For instance, it is important to provide health services and education for the citizenry. However, wanting to pay child benefit or old age pension could be counter productive where available resources and statistical data do not support such official generosity. Any government that is capable of providing jobs for its people must be honest and determined to put a regime of taxation in place. There is danger in political promises that merely dangle the carrot before the hungry.*

## Welfarism in a shrinking economy

Linda Chuba, the Member of Parliament representing a constituency of Onitsha district comes across to me as an intelligent politician who seems determined to write her name in the history books. It was a privilege to learn from her recent interview on the Minaj Broadcasting International (MBI) channel, that she had introduced a social security and welfare bill in the House of Representatives. The bill, if passed into law, will among numerous other things, result in the payment of child benefit to Nigerian parents. Such a development, she enthused, will be the real "democracy dividends" that impact on the lives of ordinary Nigerians.

No reasonable person would accuse Linda of seeking cheap popularity by proposing a bill whose outcome could benefit many Nigerian homes. If it is true, as I believe it is, that she has a scholarship scheme for people in her constituency, she would deserve to be identified as a welfarist politician who is practising what she is preaching. Welfarism is about the health, happiness and general well-being of the individual. A nation which assumes the responsibility of providing for the health, happiness and general well-being of its people(s) is regarded in political parlance as a welfare state.

Linda is not the first advocate of welfarism as a political philosophy in Nigeria. In fact, the defunct Action Group (AG), under the leadership of the late Chief Obafemi Awolowo, had injected some element of welfarism into political practice in the defunct Western Region through its "free education" and "free health" policies. The implementation of the policies was helped mainly by the enormous profits from cocoa and other agricultural resources. Chief Awolowo had proposed to introduce his welfarist policies at the national level of political governance during his campaign for national leadership in the 1959, 1979 and 1983 federal elections. One or two current political parties, it is understood, have proposed to transform Nigeria into a welfare state.

Great Britain is one example of a welfare state that is known to many Nigerians. The country upholds free health policy through its National Health Service (NHS) and various benefits are made available to its nationals. Among such benefits are those which go to senior citizens (women of 60 or over, men of 65 and over) as state pensions, unemployment benefit to the unemployed or unemployable, and benefit to every child born in Britain until he or she has attained the age of 18. Education is free to a certain level. Grants were once made available to undergraduate students for university education; however, because of a shrinking economy, prospective university students now take loans from the banks to finance their education. The most important collateral for a student loan is the letter of admission from the university and the belief that the beneficiary will be in a position to repay the loan upon graduation.

The British government, without any iota of doubt, does care for the general well-being of its citizens. Its ability to do so is helped by the co-operation of the citizens themselves. The categories of taxes paid by responsible British citizens and residents need not be detailed here. Suffice it to say that the benefits which the citizens enjoy are augmented by their own contributions. The government itself, since the dividends of colonisation have shrunk, depends on external borrowing and contributions from the European Union to sustain its philosophy of welfarism.

There is no doubt that corruption has been a great impediment to Nigeria's progress. Whether or not the country has the wherewithal to operate and sustain a full-scale welfare state is another question. Nigeria may be rich in naira terms, but when one considers the indices by which a country can be classified as rich and developing, Nigeria is far behind. One is talking of a "giant" nation that has got no national airline, where the educational system is collapsing due to lack of adequate funding, where the sick cannot be guaranteed a bed in a decent hospital, where intra-city and inter-city transportation is still poor, and where the basic skills of societal organisation are at a primitive level. A well-meaning government must focus on resolving these issues along with those of an irregular supply of electricity and water, an undependable communication network and insecurity of life and property.

Without any exaggeration, it must be said that some elements of welfare such as limited free education and fee health, are important if a nation is to realise its potential. However, governmental emphasis must focus on the diversification of the national economy and industrialisation in order to be able to meet its responsibilities to the citizenry. The citizens themselves must acknowledge that they also have a role to play in sustaining whatever benefits the dividends of democracy will be bringing to their doors.

As things are currently, if the brutal truth must be told, it would be fraudulent to promise Nigerians that every child born into their families will be entitled to state benefit. It would be fraudulent because what we have today is a nation where workers cannot be too sure that their salaries will be paid at the end of the month. In a society where many still believe that the number of children they have is the blessing of God and an aspect of their wealth, promising to pay benefits to every child born in Nigeria would be tantamount to dangling a carrot before the eyes of the hungry and playing on the ignorance of the people. The funds are simply not there for an idea whose time deserves to come.

*The Guardian, 22 October 2001*

# The Pandora's Box Of Welfarism

Let me begin this essay by stating emphatically that ours is one communal society where the hope of most parents is that the children they have laboured to provide with education would, in return, be able to support them in their old age. The fear today is the possible collapse of that cultural, social security network, not least because the jobs are hardly there for the hundreds of thousands of our young men and women who graduate yearly from colleges and universities. This is the reality that our various governments must face, rather than indulging in stirring up a hornet's nest of welfarism by creating new illusions or delusions.

Not many would fault the good intentions of the Ekiti State government to want to provide a "state pension" to citizens aged 65 and above; however, what could be faulted is its ability to sustain this scheme in the current economic state. Ekiti is one of the poorest states of the Nigerian Federation, a state that totally depends on "handouts" from Abuja for its survival. Governor Kayode Fayemi who has authored the idea of a state pension, not least because of his experience of what obtains in Great Britain where he once lived, should know that there is more to the state pension than the government appearing to be generous towards its citizens. The state pension in Great Britain is about a people reaping from contributions they have made over the years towards their future well-being. The range of taxations in Britain – income tax, national insurance, council tax, etc – if ever suggested in Nigeria - could lead to an unprecedented revolt.

A policy or philosophy of wanting to continuously share the cake we have not even learnt how to bake could be problematic in the long run. Was it not because of the new minimum wage of a meagre 18,000 (eighteen thousand) naira per month that most state governors wanted the oil subsidy removed? They argued that removing the oil subsidy would provide them with enough money to be able to pay the minimum wage. They seemed not to realise the new hardships

156

removal of the oil subsidy would also cause ordinary Nigerians who, among other things, use oil to run their generators! Those who choose to travel will experience a hike in fares.

If paying workers' salaries is still the old problem that it was, why provoke an avoidable source of expenditure that would further complicate a precarious situation. How do you even determine who has attained the age of 65, and those who have exited the payment pool, in a society where there are no records of births and deaths? Is this not the main reason why Nigeria's public registers are swelled with fictitious names? Scores of genuine pensioners, those who had served the public and paid taxes, die in long queues because physical presence is required to determine who is still alive and who is not. A friend of mine who had served his state for 38 years is yet to receive his pension of seven months!

The priority of the moment, if one must be brutally honest, should be to end the culture of corruption and deploy available resources into creating wealth for the future. What money would be left for developing our infrastructures if one generation cannot suffer for the sake of another? The various governments should be supporting small scale industries, investing in agriculture and education, with a determination to taking our young men and women off the streets and into the employment market. Our young men and women should not be made to wish for their 65th birthday to come sooner than it should!

Nigerians are a hardworking people, all they need to reveal their potential is encouragement from their various governments. Fayemi a well- admired acquaintance of mine, can lead this revolution and be a successful governor in the state we share together. Sycophants might assume this contribution to be a criticism of him, which it is not. It is an attempt by this writer to drive home the reality that confronts present day Nigeria – as he sees it.

When the various governments begin to expend the people's money in ventures they see and identify with, the moral authority will be there to remind all and sundry that taxes would have to be paid in order for us to be able to enjoy the facilities we envisage. Our peoples, just like those in the developed nations of the world, would have to make contributions that help in securing their individual and collective future. Some governments in Europe have been debating the possibility of raising the retirement age – work until you drop dead, if you can – which is to say that the state of the economy will always remain the most important factor in whether or not to dispense welfarism.

State pension, a great idea; its time could come.

*The Guardian, 27 November 2011*

# PART 8

# RELIGION AND RELIGIOSITY

## Synopsis

*Nigeria is one nation where a supposedly well-educated person could blame the breakdown of their vehicle on the evil machinations of witches, believing there would be need for prayers. The pastor or imam or priest feeds on this type of irrationality for their own economic advantages. However, the stability of Nigeria is hardly troubled by eccentric or excessive religiosity of the majority but by the determination of a very tiny minority to impose its values on the rest of society. The Nigerian state has suffered from all sorts of religious extremism in the past and is currently engaged in the battle with an extremist group whose sophistication in unleashing savagery has been unprecedented.*

## Religion: The gathering storm

The stability of Nigeria is not only threatened by rival ethnicities, but also by the fact that the country is a multi-religious state, with Christians being dominant in the South and Moslems in the North, thereby tending to exaggerate the geographical divide. The colonial administration must be held mainly responsible for this religious polarisation, because although aggressive campaigns for conversion to Christianity were encouraged in the South, European missionaries were excluded totally from the North, except in non-Moslem minority areas. It was considered unnecessary to tamper with the Islamic religion that had posed no threat to the British system of indirect rule, not least because it ensured deference to traditional suzerainty. In a letter written in 1919, the colonial office justified this position, '...because any action which weakened the authority of the Moslem religion would weaken the authority and prestige of the Emirs with the result that the present system of indirect rule would be imperilled.'

The British dualist approach resulted in educational and social imbalance between the North and South, with one axis looking up to the Middle East for inspiration and the other, the Western world. Religion has since remained a major contradiction in the Nigerian polity, not least because the first generation of leaders used it to consolidate political support in their religio-ethnic strongholds. In the 1959 federal elections, for instance, Chief Obafemi Awolowo's helicopter-assisted campaign in the North was considered offensive to Moslems with the premier of that region, Sir Ahmadu Bello, reminding northerners constantly that Awolowo was contemptuous of Islam and would ban it if he came into power. Similarly, in the South, the leadership of the country by the North was interpreted as the political expression of the *jihad* envisaged by Othman Dan Fodio, founder of the Sokoto Caliphate.

A *modus Vivendi* was sought between the two religions during the Second Republic of 1979-83 by 'balancing the ticket' between the presidential and vice presidential candidate of most of the political parties: if one were a Christian the other would be a Moslem. Further acts of balancing were consummated through the principle of 'federal character'.

In spite of the seeming incompatibility between Christianity and Islam as practised in some parts of Nigeria, the adherents of each faith continued to live side by side in reasonable harmony until a 'new apparent danger' in their peaceful co-existence was ignited by the insurrection of the Maitasine fundamentalists in December 1980, when several hundred were killed in Kano as a result of the clashes with the army and police. In spite of the ruthless response to the sect's wanton destruction, further outbreaks of violence took place in Maiduguri, Yola, and Gombe between 1982 and 1983.

A greater threat to the stability of the nation came one year later in the Northern states, mainly in Kaduna, when Islamic fanatics went on the rampage and burned down various churches and other Christian properties. The rioting was clearly a great embarrassment to the incumbent military ruler, General Ibrahim Babangida who described it as 'equivalent of a civil coup', and in June 1987 he established an Advisory Council on Religious Affairs that had a membership of 12 Moslems and 12 Christians.

On three important occasions the issue of religion *vis-à-vis* the secularity of the state provoked heated public controversies that have transcended Nigeria's north-south parameter. The debates in the Constituent Assembly during 1978 about a federal *Sharia* court of appeal saw the non-Moslem leaders in the former northern region allying with politicians from the south, and in the end section 242(1) of the 1979 Constitution provided for state *Sharia* courts of appeal. In 1983, President Shehu Shagari provoked a hostile reaction from Christians when he was about to establish a Department of Islamic Affairs in his presidency. And, in January 1986, the Babangida Government was taken to task over its decision to recognise Nigeria's membership of the Organisation of Islamic Conference.

The issue of Sharia once again heated up in 1988, when another Constituent Assembly, with as many as 567 members (450 elected and 117 nominated) met to discuss the constitution that would create the Third Republic in 1992. Committee 16 failed to arrive at a decision about Sharia because the Moslem members wanted to upgrade its status by establishing a federal court of appeal, while the Christian members (equal in number) wanted it to be expunged from the constitution. The acrimony generated by the heated debate was such that public peace was threatened, and the government intervened by banning any further discussion since, according to Babangida, 'the issue had already been settled in the 1979 Constitution. That is the bottom line.'

All these developments indicate that religious tensions were not far from the surface. In 1987, Sheikh Abubakar Gumi warned that future politics could be based on religion. Appraising Babangida's proposed 'two-party system', the Islamic scholar predicted that it would lead to a Christian-Moslem divide, rather than polarise on a north-south basis. He was of the view that Moslems would not tolerate a Christian leader of the Federal Government: such a person could be appointed 'by use of force or by army coup but by election it would be difficult for (a) non-Moslem to be leader in Nigeria be election'. And when asked what would happen if Christians refused to accept Moslem leadership, Gumi replied, 'then we have to divide the country'.

The outspoken Bishop of Lagos believed that Alhaji Gumi had not spoken for himself, and in his reactions to the latter's statements, Dr. A.O. Okogie warned that the Christians would burn the country. Said the Bishop, 'we just want to keep Nigeria because of peace but if anybody tried any nonsense this time, I don't care, we will burn the nation because it is going to be a religious war and nobody will dare stop anybody, no gun will stop it.' As explained by General Olusegun Obasanjo, in his capacity as former Head of State, 'by act of commission we have raised the religious issue to a high pedestal. We can neither sweep it under the carpet nor ignore it. We must face the issue squarely and permanently lay it to rest.'

Now that the issue of Sharia has resurfaced in its most naked form, thereby re-awakening the slumbering religious tension in the country, the great task has ironically fallen to President Olusegun Obasanjo whose administration must now lay the issue of religion permanently to rest.

Is Sharia aimed at destabilising his government, simply because he is a Christian who happened to have been elected as the political leader of Nigeria? The statement credited to Alhaji Gumi suggests that this could be so, and many commentators who have questioned the motives of the current development by asking why Sharia was not such a disturbing issue under erstwhile Moslem Heads of State (Shagari, Buhari, Babangida and Abacha) would seem to be nodding to that. It must, however, be said that the election which produced

162

Obasanjo as president was contested by two candidates of the same religious persuasion. Both Moslems and Christians participated actively in determining the outcome.

Or, is it that the state governments implementing the Islamic legal system are merely responding to the wishes of the majority of their electorate? The view that they are has been credited to former leaders, Shehu Shagari and Muhammadu Buhari in their various statements on the controversial issue. Vice-President Alhaji Atiku Abubakar has recently joined the fold of leaders who believe that the implementation of Sharia was a response to the democratic demands in the affected states. The history of the struggle to force Sharia into the national constitution by Constituent Assembly delegates would also suggest that the adherents might just be seizing the opportunity of a democratic atmosphere to do what they had always wanted to do.

States, in a true federation, have powers to make laws with regards to order and good governance within their areas of legislative jurisdiction. In the United States of America, for instance, some states have the death penalty for capital offences, whereas some do not. The diversity and autonomy of the American states are such that tourists are advised to read as much as they can about the states they are visiting as thee rules and regulations change from one border to the other. However, in none of the American states is the law based on religion.

The introduction of the Islamic legal system into some states of the north is the most divisive development since colonialism. It is a product of the British dualist approach to religion which, invariably, affected educational growth in that region. With a leadership that is unable to redirect the course of history, Nigeria has ever since been a nation at cross-purposes with itself – a nation of divided ambition, interests and (I hope not) future.

*The Guardian, 27 July 2000*

163

# The Future Of Nigeria

"Our boys will defeat them" was what one Nigerian said rather dismissively when told that Ghana was winning one-mil at half-time in the semi-final of the African Cup of Nations. He seemed to have forgotten that Nigeria needed to find an equalising goal before the prospect of winning the match could be realistically assumed. The Nigerian in question had merely exhibited our typical attitude of under-estimating others – assuming ourselves to have got to a destination we are not in any way near.

Assuming ourselves to have gone beyond a point we may not have reached could be dangerous particularly in politics. It could mean we are unreasonable or unrealistic. For instance, when Barack Obama won the American presidency in November 2008 there were some calling for the removal of those "gadgets" that kept our fragile nation together. One prominent Nigerian was reported as saying that the federal character principle was no longer relevant because the election of Barack Obama suggested we could do without it.

The problem with this naivety is the assumption that we are at the same stage of political development as the United States of America. We may actually not have been where they were 60 years ago. A more blunt individual might say we are 100 years behind them. Is it not a fact of our contemporary history that some Nigerians still do not believe in the importance of Western education? Is it also not a fact that the nation we have today is one in which a significant population of our peoples cannot converse among themselves except through an interpreter?

The truth of the matter is that Nigeria is yet to meet the yardsticks of a true nation. Nigeria may only marginally have advanced beyond being the "mere geographical expression" Chief Obafemi Awolowo rightly called it very many years ago. True acknowledgement of how far we have gone in history is the way forward to getting to how far we may wish to go.

Religion, for instance, should be a private matter – not the cause of the deaths of hundreds of our peoples on a periodic basis. The truth of the matter is that many of us could have been Hindus today if India, assumingly, were the nation that colonised us! Religion does not call for the type of madness that has become our lot. Sadly, the nation we have today is one in which peaceful co-existence cannot be taken for granted. There are parents warning their loved ones not to seek opportunities in some areas of a society they call their own.

The advantages of a united Nigerian nation cannot be over-emphasised. However, the assumption that the future of such an entity is great for all of us should not be at the expense of innocent lives. Our political and religious leaders must embark on educating our peoples about the advantage of a peaceful and orderly Nigerian society. Such an education is important and urgent, especially in the wild north.

There can be no meaningful development where politics is more important than governance. There is too much politics and too little governance in Nigeria and one explanation for this may be the absence of a realistic Constitution. Debates in the past two months have been about an absentee president not delegating authority to his deputy. While the ethnic factor cannot be ignored , it will nevertheless be unfortunate if the stubbornness or selfishness of President Umaru Yar'Adua is responsible for this. Until we acknowledge the dangers posed by our cleavages and work out a political arrangement that accommodates the sentiments of our peoples, the omen would always remain ominous for our society.

There may be occasions when one admires the naivety of others, especially when such a naivety is in itself an expression of hope and patriotism. One with limited knowledge of Nigerian history could be pardoned for concluding that Nigerians have never cared about where their political leader comes from. Of course one should not care about such a thing if one Mr Goodluck Jonathan from a minority ethnic group is afforded the same opportunity, respect and legitimacy as one Alhaji Umaru Yar'Adua from a majority ethnic group. The series of crises we have experienced in our history might not have occurred if such a desirable thing as this had always been taken for granted.

The leadership question is a psychological one, which makes it all the more difficult. However, the totality of society is responsible for its development or lack of it. A political leader with the best of intentions can be frustrated by an irresponsible legislature or judiciary. Similarly a responsible legislature or judiciary can bring out the best of an otherwise mediocre leadership. Who, for instance, is responsible for the failure to amend the Constitution or introduce reforms that have been suggested a couple of years ago? How many Nigerians can boast of having confronted their elected men and women about their individual and collective expectations since 1999? It is because we are all involved that one is posing these questions.

We must learn to respect each other. The small ethnic group deserves as much respect as the majority one, the latter not being dismissive of the former as we did of Ghana in that crucial semi-final football match. The small ethnic group or nation has its own strength and determination which the so-called majority group underestimate at its own peril. Respect for one another ensures there are no unwanted surprises – surprises whose consequences may be difficult to reverse. The future of Nigeria can be great if we work honestly towards it.

*The Guardian,08 February 2010*

# The complex terrain of religion

The aim here is to bring two recent publications – a book and a journal article – to the attention of those interested in theology. This, however, will be preceded by an attempt to clarify a statement this writer made in a recent article – a clarification now compelled by a friendly rejoinder from an enthusiastic reader.

In the said article, 'The Future of Nigeria', (The Guardian, February 8 2010) the writer stated that "most of us could have been Hindus today if India, assumingly, were the nation that colonised us". What one was trying to emphasise by that statement was that neither Christianity nor Islam was indigenous to those who uphold them in the various communities.

Both Islam and Christianity came by way of conquest, persuasion or cajoling. Any other religion could have come and been embraced via similar routes if our historical experiences had been any different from what they were.

Hence the religious madness that pervades our society today is uncalled for. The civilized world cannot understand the type of hatred that would have provoked a people to murder their own in hundreds, as has recently been the case in plateau State. The fact that this has not been a one-off incident makes it all the more worrying. The argument has always been that people were manipulated into committing crimes of this nature by those who have vested interests. The question is: what kind of people can be manipulated to do things they would not ordinarily have done of their own accord?

Education is very important and a people should have a reason for wanting to live. With mass poverty and unemployment co-existing with the gluttonous greed of a tiny minority, the future is bleak for our society. Any government that genuinely wants to curtail sectarian conflicts must provide meaningful education and jobs for its own people. Education cures ignorance, while proper education chisels out the crude edges in all of us. And, of course, commensurate punishment must be inflicted on anyone who chooses to violate the law of the land. The culture of impunity tends to be encouraged when violators of public peace and order go unpunished. There should be no sacred cows but scapegoats!

Now, turning to the two useful publications one is so excited to bring to the attention of interested readers. Twentieth Century Theologians (I.B.Tauris, 2010) is written by Dr (Rev) Phillip Kennedy, a lecturer of theology and Senior Research Fellow at Mansfield College, University of Oxford. The book discusses a variety of theologians within a specific region of the world. One should therefore not be surprised if the great theologians of the African continent do not feature in this interesting book. Dr Kennedy defines a theologian as "someone who tries to talk about God". In an argument that would suggest that the 'Okija priest' or the 'Osun priestess' or even the atheist is also a theologian, the author has this to say about 'God' as a concept, "…whether there is one God or several gods cannot be ascertained with certainty by human intelligence. It is not even clear what or to whom the noun 'God' refers, or whether it designates a reality in or beyond the world…" There might have been a time in history when some inquisitor might have considered a statement such as this as 'heresy' but not anymore in the civilised world where diverse ideas compete and contend. The assumption that there could be one God, or the same God in different perceptions provides a most welcome intrusion of the seminal article written by Professor Moses Olobatuyi of the Department of Sociology, Morgan State University. His article entitled, 'The Social Relevance of Yoruba Traditional Religion: Olosunta, the "Orun Ikere"', published by the Lincoln Journal of Social and Political Thought, Vol.6 No.2, 2009, argues that 'Olosunta', erstwhile popular deity of the Ikere people, has relevance in modern religions. His detailed exposition of the history of Ikere and the evolution of its traditional institutions should be of interest to those who seek further understanding of their own environment. Professor Moses Olobatuyi, if one may introduce him formally here, is one Nigerian scholar who has argued consistently for cultural revivalism. He is of the opinion that while culture is relative and no culture can claim to be superior to another, a people who copy other cultures with relish portray theirs as inferior. While acknowledging that culture itself is not static, he nevertheless bemoans the fact that we tend to copy more from the Western world than they do from us. He identifies the family system, especially the love and concern for the aged, as a superior aspect of African culture. The African, according to him, would rather have their old ones live and die at home than abandon them to carers in 'Old People's Homes'!

Dr Olobatuyi is also of the view that a people should know and celebrate their history. 'Thanksgiving Day', for instance, is undoubtedly the most important day in America's calendar. What brings Thanksgiving about in America has historical similarities with 'Idupe' in Ikere – Ekiti. Both are about war exploits and the establishment of the state or community as it currently is. 'Idupe', which means 'thanksgiving', is an annual ceremony held at the Oba's palace in honour of Ikere's war chiefs. While all Americans, including religious leaders, enthusiastically celebrate and enjoy 'Thanksgiving Day', there are confused, overzealous individuals who dismiss the Ikere occasion as anachronistic or even anti-God.

There are, in fact, many so-called educated men and women who do not know the history of the occasion! So much for the confusion colonisation has injected into our psyches!

What one must, however, try to grasp from older, stable nations, is what is universal to humanity. Democracy, for instance, is not just about electing politicians into political offices, it is about a people enjoying the basic opportunities of freedom, albeit within the purview of the law. Such basic opportunities include freedom of speech, choice and association. It should, for instance, be taken for granted that the legitimate choice we make, be it of religion, is accepted and respected by those whose choices may be different. Those who seek to propagate democracy as a culture must accept that their most important, and perhaps equally difficult, task is to establish a tolerant state – a state where we can successfully navigate the complex terrain of religion or ethnicity without anyone getting injured or going missing!

*The Guardian, 15 March 2010*

# Religion and the flying pastors

Two athletes, one African and one British, were interviewed after the successful conclusion of their respective events. The African who had won an event attributed her success to the grace of God. "He touched my limbs; I could not have done it without him." The British athlete, on the other hand, gave substantial credit to her coach as she attributed her success to a regime of rigorous training.

Of course glory must be given to God for all we are able to achieve as mortal human beings. There are certain things we are never going to achieve in life either because we are too tall or too short! The natural attributes which propel us to unimaginable heights can hardly be purchased in the cosmetic market. However, our natural attributes or talents could be a waste if not augmented by appropriate training. In short, there is something to be celebrated in the explanations both athletes attributed to their individual successes.

Those of us exposed to cultures other than our own have exciting stories about the gulf of differences in cultures. The British man or woman may be quite happy to say "Happy New Year" to you but cannot understand why you need to keep praying for what you would like God to do for them in the New Year. He or she knows, for instance, that to own a home one would have to approach a bank for a mortgage!

There is this temptation on my part to assume or conclude that the British, for instance, may be more rational than the Nigerian. This writer is hardly the most rational of human beings, so there is an element of self-criticism here! Even among the British who go to church there is hardly the punctuation of every conceivable sentence with "in Jesus name" as is common among Nigerian Christians. They believe that a lot of problems can be resolved without having to involve Jesus in them. One sometimes wonders if Britain was indeed the nation that introduced Christianity to Nigeria, not least because the life of the typical British person is no longer dominated by religion.

I think I have a perspective into the Christian religion as is currently practiced in Nigeria and this perspective came from a discussion with a Nigerian lady who once told me that "people have their different reasons for going to church". I tried to argue that there is only one universal reason why people should go to church, to worship God and assimilate the Christian culture and that the blessings of the Lord, either here or in heaven, come with devotion to the cause. Wanting to win an election, or an anxiety to be promoted at work, should not be the motivating factor for wanting to go to church. Unfortunately the Nigerian lady was talking from experience which, in itself, explains why many Nigerians have become vulnerable to exploitation in the hands of fake pastors who claim to have divine power for all sorts of problems.

The Nigerian early churches were what the Church still is in some societies. The priest prays with and for the congregation without claiming to have the power to reveal what lies ahead. Many Nigerians want to know what the future holds for them and they also seek miracles. Otherwise, how do you explain the fact that some Nigerians phone home to ask their pastors to pray for their visas to be extended here in Britain? We are a people cocooned in ignorance and that is the major problem.

The Christian Church has been great to Nigeria, especially the southern part of it. Of course Christianity came with colonisation but society in general has not been the worse for it. The achievements of the early missionaries are well documented and such achievements can be seen in the areas of education and health. It can be said without much contradiction that Christianity has contributed substantially to the foundation of our society.

The Church continues to play a prominent part in development. Even a few recent churches have established universities of relatively good quality. The Church must continue to make its presence felt in areas of community development, as well as in improving the morals of our peoples. The Nigerian nation, sadly, is one of the most corrupt in the world - something of an irony for a nation which undoubtedly is also one of the most religious. The Church, therefore, has an ideological responsibility to engage in the war against corruption and a moral one to discourage materialism and ostentatious living which Jesus Christ himself so much detested in the predispositions of the Pharisees.

Is the perception of the Christian Church as a vanguard of morality well represented by pastors flying all over the place in private jets while most of their flock go about hungry and bare footed? I tried to appraise the issue of some Nigerian pastors and their private gets with an open mind - bad roads and long distances to travel - but a British theologian seemed to have convinced me that "it is not the way to propagate the gospel". The trend we are witnessing is towards the culture of those boisterous American pastors who tend to explain every big thing they have - houses, cars and yachts - as the favour of God. It will be sad if Nigerians now aspire to the leadership of the Church, as they do in politics, solely because it is perceived as an avenue leading to influence and flamboyance.

*The Guardian, 06 April 2009*

# PART 9

# FEDERALISM AND THE CONSTITUTION

## SYNOPSIS

*There would have been no need for a nation to be federal if it were not one made up of people with different values and backgrounds. The problem in Nigeria has always been the assumption that unity and uniformity are interchangeable when it comes to the organization of state and society. The nature of state federal relations does not support that assumption in the most successful federal nations of the world, especially the United States of America where the federal ideology originated. The argument for the restructuring of Nigerian federation can hardly be contradicted if containing ethnic and religious tensions were indeed a priority.*

## Reviewing the Constitution

Nigerian democracy can continue to benefit from experiences elsewhere. The resignation of Thabo Mbeki as president of South Africa should have informed us that respect for the principles of democracy is a lot more honourable than the crudeness of our own approach. Were Thabo Mbeki the typical Nigerian leader, he probably would have dispatched trucks full of Naira notes to the residences of party elders with a view to buying their loyalty. Alternatively, a state of civil disorder would be his option.

And what of recent events in the United States of America? George W. Bush did not bribe lawmakers to approve his rescue bill. Even when not much is going to change immediately in that great nation except the impending replacement of Mr Bush as president, the twists and turns over the $700 billion bailout of Wall Street provides a lesson in the workings of the principle of Separation of Powers.

Is it not remarkable that the initial headache President Bush encountered over his bailout proposal was from members of his own Republican Party? The representatives face re-election in November and listening to the views of their own constituents is the only way by which their return to Congress can be assured. When it is said that American lawmakers have independent voting behaviours, it is a combination of personal principles as well as pressure from those who elected them into office. It is exactly this type of independent voting behaviour that one wishes for our Nigerian representatives.

The members of America's House of Representatives are elected for two years and expected to be energetic men and women whose primary desire is to serve constituent interests. However, lawmakers in the Senate are expected to be mature men and women motivated by concerns of national interest over and above parochial local interests. The reason the founding fathers approved a term of six years for senators is that such a generous tenure would take the pressure of non-election out of their systems. It should be recollected that George Bush's not-too-popular bailout of the greedy banks endured less opposition in the Senate than it did in the House. However, it was considered a matter of national interest to bailout the failed banks.

The principle of Separation of Powers does not work in a vacuum; it works because people make it work. Nigerians must learn how to influence the outcome of political decisions by putting pressure on those they have elected into various levels of political governance. If it is the national interest for a bill to be passed into law, concerned Nigerians at the grassroots should be able to meet with elected representatives and tell them where they expect their votes to go. The reason the representatives are paid constituency allowances from taxpayers' money is to facilitate continued interaction with those who elected them into office. Any representative who cannot respect the dominant position in his or her constituency should not deserve to be re-elected in a future election. Nigerians must be involved in legislative processes because the Gani Fawehimis and the Press cannot be left alone to contend with democratic responsibilities that belong to all of us.

The legislative arm of government has a special significance of its own. It is hoped that a future Nigerian legislature will be able to boast of capable men and women whose experiences in representation and lawmaking have blossomed by virtue of their long tenancies in that area of government. What obtains in the United States of America is a Congress where there are members who have served their constituencies for decades and the records are there to reveal how they have voted on pertinent issues over the years. The legislative arm of government should not be a factory for temporary employees!

The indication that the Nigerian Constitution is about to be reviewed compels a re-statement of earlier suggestions here. The writer believes fervently that future elections can benefit the principle of Separations of Powers as well as the orderliness of its own conduct if staggered. This, in itself, will necessitate our tinkering with the terms of office current elected politicians enjoy. What about the retention of four years for members of the House of Representatives, a new six-year term for senators and a single term of six or seven years for presidents? The single-term presidency is particularly strongly recommended and the observation of incumbent President Umaru Yar'Adua that rotation of the presidency has brought peace to Nigeria can only be dismissed out of hand by those who are not familiar with the history of our great nation. The ruling People's Democratic Party (PDP) endorses the idea.

There is this lazy assumption that a two-party system can be achieved by limiting political competition to only two political parties. Of course it is desirable that we have a manageable number of parties but the philosophy of 'if you disagree with Party A there is no other place to go other than party B' is one gimmick of the Babangida era that this writer vehemently opposed. The reason we have tended to have too many political parties is because every Nigerian wants to be president at the same time.


Once we have entrenched the principle of leadership rotation in the Constitution, the party system will develop its characters and crystallise as democracy takes root in our society. The broad-based political party, as experience in Europe and America informs us, is an amalgam of diverse ideological viewpoints and political temperaments. It cannot be otherwise in the Nigerian nation of about 140 million people with varied background.

What we must develop quickly is the culture of free and fair elections, tolerance for competing viewpoints as well as loyalty to whatever principles we claim to have embraced. How can there be a two-party system when the prevailing attitude among Nigerians is that of wanting to be identified with whatever political party is in power? Dreams belong to the future; there are great things we wish for Nigeria, which we may not necessarily achieve during our own lifetimes. However, we must create an enabling environment that makes the dreams we dream realisable for future Nigerians.

*The Guardian 16 October 2008*

# UNSOLVED PROBLEMS OF FEDERALISM

NIGERIA is a unique federal nation. William H. Riker describes this country of various languages, customs and religions as the only one of the ex-British federations that was not created by the unification of a number of separate colonies none of which was viable alone. Therefore it can be argued that the problem of integration in Nigeria is largely the problem of ensuring peaceful coexistence among nationalities, which, by virtue of their populations and territorial exclusiveness, are capable of existing as viable, independent nations.

Nigeria is still an evolving federal nation. The eminent historian professor A.E. Afigbo has attempted to explain the development of Nigerian federalism in three stages, viz (1) the period of informal federation, 1900-1946; (2) the first period of formal federation, 1946-1965, and (3) the second period of formal federation, 1967 to date. A cursory excursion into these outlined stages is crucial to understanding what successes Nigeria has made, and what further steps need to be taken in order to ensure that the most populous African nation becomes a true, stable federal nation.

The period of informal federation was the era when the government of Nigeria could at best be described as quasi-federal. The British imperialists recognised the diversity of the Nigerian nation and the eventual birth of the country in 1914 was achieved through the progressive merger of colonies. From 1900 to 1946, Nigeria was more or less governed as two administrative units; the Northern and Southern Nigeria Protectorates. The historic tripartite arrangement of North, East and West came into being when the Southern Nigeria Protectorate was bifurcated into East and West in 1939.

The lack of sufficient effort on the part of the British colonialists to achieve a united nation was evident first in the system of Indirect Rule, which was employed in governing the administrative units and secondly in the activities of missionaries whose evangelistic crusades were limited to the so-called pagan areas, i.e. the south and the minority ethnic group areas of the north. The outcome was the emergence of a nation whose north is dominated by Muslims and its south by Christians. A south with greater advancement in Western education and values viewed the north as conservative and primitive, while the latter's impression of the former was equally uncomplimentary. The authors of its creation had thus sowed the mutual distrust and disrespect, which characterised the relationship between the different axes of the Nigerian polity.

However, the Nigerian nation made a further advance in 1946 when Sir Arthur Richards came up with a proposal to bring Nigeria under one administrative set-up. Although Nigeria did not formally become a federation until 1954 when the Lyttelton constitution was adopted, the concepts of North, East and West had become firmly rooted, not only in the administrative governance of the country but also in its perception, both within and without, as a nation of the Hausa-Fulani, Igbo and Yoruba, who, respectively, were the dominant nationalities in the three regions. Support for the three major political parties, the Northern Peoples Congress (NPC), National Council of Nigerian Citizens (NCNC) and Action Group (AG), revolved mainly around the major nationalities.

The minority ethnic groups sought relevance in their own political parties which agitated the creation of states but their aspirations were frustrated by the selfishness of the majority ethnic groups - a selfishness demonstrated by the non-implementation of the Willink Commission's report of 1958 which recommended the creation of new states as a way of allaying the fears of the minority ethnic groups. The vision-less post-independence civilian government did create the Mid-Western Region in 1963; but rather than solving a national problem, this was more of an opportunity on the part of the NPC/NCNC government to curtail the influence of the recalcitrant AG, the leading party in opposition.

The "messiah" of the minority ethnic nationalities came in the person of Lt. Col. (as he was then) Yakubu Gowon, the third Nigerian Head of State. His predecessor, Major-General J.T.U. Aguiyi-Ironsi, had misguidedly transformed Nigeria into a unitary state by his unification decree no 34 on May 24, 1966. The implications of Unitarianism were not lost on the relatively underdeveloped north whose key leaders had just been killed in a coup (January 15, 1966) engineered mainly by young Igbo officers. They mounted a hostile revolt against Ironsi and his Igbo compatriots. Ironsi was killed in a bloody coup on July 29, 1966. Gowon, on assuming power, immediately reverted Nigeria to its erstwhile arrangement. He was himself a member of a minority ethnic group in the North and the prospect of secession by the Eastern Region hastened his decision to demarcate Nigeria into 12 states in 1967. Thus Gowon achieved what prominent politicians and political activists from the minority ethnic groups had failed to achieve through decades of persuasion and violent agitation, through a decree. Professor Afigbo sees the importance of Gowon's regime in the development of the Nigerian federation "in the fact that it enabled the fundamental character of the Nigerian federation, that is its multi-ethnic character; to emerge full and defiant as well as naked, repulsive and challenging. Hitherto it had tended to be obscured by British-generated cleavages between mere geographical expressions such as between first, North and South and then among North, East and West."

Gowon's landmark achievement was carried further by three of his military successors, Generals Murtala Mohammed (1975-76), Ibrahim Babangida (1983-93) and Sani Abacha (1993-98). In spite of the fact that Nigeria has been transformed into a federation of 36 states, calls for its restructuring have persisted, suggestions have been made for the adoption of confederation as an alternative political arrangement. Discontent with the state of the Nigerian federation has tended to be expressed mainly in the south, lop-sidedness in the distribution of political and military power providing the platform for new agitations and strategies.

The creation of states must go down as the military's most important contribution to the development of Nigerian federation. However, debate has since shifted from that sphere to the nature of power relationships, first between state and the federal government, and secondly among the component units of the Nigerian federation - a debate long suppressed by the military's unitary approach to political governance - has assumed many dimensions since the re-emergence of democratic rule in May 1999.

What would seem to be the most blatant attempt to assert state autonomy vis-Ã-vis the centre came in the introduction of the Sharia legal system into some states of the North. Opponents of Sharia have imputed various motives for this development, but it must be said that Sharia has always been an issue in the Nigerian federation. It has always been a contradiction, which was bound to develop into a major one once the country became a democracy, and it has done so at a great loss in human lives and inter-ethnic relations. Sharia would appear to have come to stay in the states that opted for it. A challenge to its method of operation would have to come from those directly affected by its operation.

Another dominant issue is that of the control of revenue accruing from resources located in the various states of the federation. With the decline of export-geared agriculture, about ninety per cent of Nigeria's foreign exchange accrues from oil resources. The oil-producing states of the south want a greater share in revenue allocation, while the most militant of their population want outright control over the resources. The approval of 13 per cent revenue allocation to the oil-producing states may have reduced tension to a reasonable extent, but the issue of revenue allocation will always remain a contentious one. The reason why it is not a serious crisis may have to do with the fact that the majority of oil resources are located in the territories of the minority ethnic groups.

Perhaps the development, which has the most disturbing prospects for the future of the Nigerian federation is the resurgence of ethnic and regional associations, on the scale of the ones witnessed in pre-independence Nigeria. The most prominent have been the Oodua Peoples Congress (OPC) representing the Yoruba, the Arewa Peoples Congress (APC) which seeks to re-invent an "indivisible" North, and the Ohaneze N'digbo, which is an association determined to promote Igbo interests within or outside the Nigerian federation. The activities of these organisations, which need not be detailed here, have been highlighted in various reports. They are most disturbing, not least because key leaders of the various ethnicities would appear to believe that their ethnic organisations are more important than the Nigerian nation. For instance, five former Nigerian leaders who hail from the North (Yakubu Gowon, Shehu Shagari, Muhammadu Buhari, Ibrahim Babangida and Absulsalami Abubakar) were conspicuously absent from the celebrations that marked the fortieth anniversary of Nigeria's independence from colonial rule; the Arewa organisation had accused the incumbent president, Olusegun Obasanjo, of marginalising the North in the scheme of things. Recently a meeting of the southern governors was held in Lagos; among other things, they agreed to fight jointly for a new revenue allocation arrangement that will enhance autonomy and resource control by the constituent units of the Nigerian federation.

What is to be done? The potential is there for the disintegration of the Nigerian federation, as happened to federations like the Soviet Union, Czechoslovakia and Yugoslavia. Nigeria's main ethnic groups have their own exclusive territories; it would only require disillusionment on a massive scale to put an end to what the British colonialists cobbled together in 1914. However, the advantages of a big African nation with substantial influence in international politics and regional affairs are overwhelming.

The assumption that uniformity and unity are two interchangeable words has been the undoing of the Nigerian society. It would appear that the time is now ripe for discussions about how to manage a new Nigerian nation in the form of a loose federation in which the component units are permitted to express themselves in their own peculiar ways. This would entail the devolution of powers from the central government to the state or regional governments in generally agreed areas. For instance the police could be regionalised in order for it to enforce those laws that are unique to the different component units of the federation, while the military continues to play the unifying role it was designed to play as a national institution. The suggestion being made in some quarters for the regionalisation of the military is, in my considered opinion, a recipe for the break-up of the Nigerian federation.

Discussions must also centre on the institution of national leadership, which has been the source of inter-ethnic conflict since Nigeria became independent in 1960. My view is that the American Presidential model is most inappropriate to Nigeria because the complexities that make it a success in America differ substantially from Nigeria's unique circumstances.

*West Africa,30 November 2000*

# The Problem of Democracy and Constitution-Making

One definition of democracy which has become universal and unambiguous is that provided by Abraham Lincoln as "the government of the people, by the people, for the people". Democracy itself, as a culture, originated from Greece where it was the practice in those days for people to assemble in public places and arrive at decisions through popular acclamation. However, democracy has gone through evolution as society and the governmental process have become all the more complex. Today, democracy is not just the dictatorship of the majority, but an activity that is governed by a set of agreed rules and procedures. Such rules and procedures are stated in a legal document called "the Constitution".

Principally because Nigeria is a federal nation whose current constitution is patterned after the American presidential/congressional system, a brief excursion into the constitutional history of the United States may help in raising one or two questions about the Nigerian situation. Suffice to say that prior to the Connecticut Convention of 1787 the United States of America was a confederacy of 13 independent colonies. The constitution of 1787 transformed it into a federal nation which, today, boasts of 50 states. The new states that bolstered the original 13 colonies were either purchased or admitted into the union. By 2007, the American Constitution will be 220 years old.

The point one is trying to make here is that America has had only one constitutional convention in its entire history and produced only one constitution which has enjoyed a few amendments over the years as it continues to adapt to modern changes, whereas the history of Nigeria is littered with periodic constitutional conferences and constitution-making. The Clifford Constitution of 1922, the Richards Constitution of 1945, the Lyttleton Constitution of 1953, were some of the constitutions that celebrated the era of British colonialists in the pre-independence era. Since independence in 1960, we have had a catalogue of constitutions and constitutional conferences. There was the 1963 constitution which met its untimely death in the military coup d'etat of January 1966. Since that unfortunate episode, most military dictators had dished one constitution or the other in commemoration of their rule. The Nigerian law-makers are currently working on what could be a new constitution and their invention may not be the last if the sole intention is to achieve a transient, selfish ambition of a "third term" for the incumbent President of the Federal Republic.

The main problem with constitution-making in Nigeria is one that derives from the structure of the society itself. If the definition of a nation as an entity that comprises a people with common ancestry, common culture and a common language is anything to go by, then Nigeria does not qualify to be called a nation. However, Nigeria is a country that owes its origin to British empire-builders who, for their own designs, amalgamated nations of different peoples into a single entity. The story of constitution-making in Nigeria has therefore been the story of a post-colonial nation searching for a bearing.

What many nations of the world have, which we do not have in Nigeria, is what can be called a "common destiny". The style and approach of British administration and governance has its own portion of the blame. But it must be said that since independence in 1960, the ambition of one group to predominate over other(s) has been a major clog in the wheel of nation-building. Issues of state creation and census, which, ordinarily, would have advanced the cause of national unity, national integration and development, were viewed from the prisms of ethnic advantage. The most recent constitutional conference, the 2005 Olusegun Obasanjo-sponsored National Political Reform Conference, further testifies to the fact that even contemporary Nigerians have not weaned themselves off petty ethnic jealousies. Maybe it is an incontrovertible political fact that ethnic groups are in perpetual conflict with one another, as one group tends to measure its progress in society against those of others. Even the small matter of presidential tenure split the Nigerian constitutionalists along the historic North versus South divide.

184

However, the optimism that Nigeria will survive its ordeals and transform into a great African nation with immense global influence is not unfounded. The nation may be driving at a snail's pace but it has not been static. There is one piece of good news and that is that most Nigerians believe in the future of their society. It cannot but be noticed that quality opposition to President Olusegun Obasanjo's alleged third term scheming has been coming from his own ethnic background. Their respect for constitutionality and lack of ambition for ethnic hold on political power should provide all of us with the important lesson that federalism after all is about "give and take".

The problem of democracy cannot be divorced from that of constitution-making, as there is also the attitudinal or behavioural element to the endemic corruption and the culture of election rigging which have not aided the cause of democracy anywhere in the world. Even when the mission is to establish their own greed, it is on record that the soldiers who terminated democratic rules in the past had attempted to explain their actions by the corruption of politicians and their failure to respect the electoral verdict of the people. Most of Nigeria's elected politicians fear life outside political office and defeat at the polls is one "disgrace" they find difficult to contemplate.

Greedy politicians feed on mass illiteracy and societal poverty. The level of political education and participation in Nigeria is rather low, even when its press is arguably one of the most vibrant in the world. Not many are aware of the bills being debated in the various legislative houses, talk less of wanting to influence their outcome by putting pressure on their elected representatives. A member of the Federal House of Representatives when asked why legislators were demanding increased constituency allowances, said each time they visited their constituencies the people expected to be fed. He went on to enumerate the market prices of a ram and that of a bag of rice and that, itself, speaks volumes about the Nigerian society.

But it must be quickly warned that democracy is a late developer, a culture that requires sufficient time before it can take root. The one thing Nigerians must be determined not to permit is another interruption by the military. With time, Nigerians will be proud to say "ours is a truly democratic nation".

*The Guardian 29 March 2006*

# PART 10

# BETWEEN OPTIMISM AND PESSIMISM

## SYNOPSIS

*Most Nigerians are proud of their nation and share the hope that it could be one of the most important nations in the world. However, there tends to be tension and despair in the periods of crisis. The truth of the matter is that many great nations had experienced difficult stages of history and that should be the inspiration or consolation for the patriotic ones that are still in the majority. The year 2015 is significant ----not because of the self seeking prediction that Nigeria would break-up------because it is another putative presidential election year and such an important election tends to assume inter ethnic or North versus South dimensions.*

## Peaceful Co-Existence Remains a dream

The participants may have cultivated the habit of interrupting one another rather crudely, but this has not in any way diminished the usefulness of the discussion panel hosted by Gbenga Aruleba on the African International Television channel. A recent discussion of great interest was on whether or not the geo-political zones created by the government of the late General Sani Abacha in 1995 should be accorded a constitutional recognition. An exciting contribution came from a lady who said she could not stand people wanting to know where she came f rom, although she introduced herself as a Nigerian from Ile-Oluji in Ondo State.

187

Wanting to know where one comes from should be one standard question taken for granted on meeting another person for the first time. It is not uncommon in the western world to hear people say, "my parents were from Pakistan, but I was born in London", or "I was originally from New York but now I am a Washingtonian". In fact people proudly wear T-shirts with the names of their cities or towns inscribed on them. There would have been no reason for the lady from Ile-Oluji not to enthusiastically flaunt her place of birth if ours were not a society where danger and disadvantages await "unwelcome sojourners".

That cartoon depicting the Holy Prophet Mohammed rather derogatorily was unnecessary. The author and the newspaper that published the cartoon had intended to insult Islam, but what they never intended were the consequences of their stupid action. There were understandable reactions and protests in most cities of the world, such protests directed at the embassies of countries where the cartoon had been published. What one cannot appreciate is why, in Nigeria, we went the extra mile of taking revenge on our own people. Nigeria's protesters did not converge on Abuja and Lagos and make their anger known to the officials of the foreign countries where the cartoon had been published; instead, what was reported on radio and in the newspapers was that 51 Nigerians were killed and churches burnt down in Maiduguri by religious protesters. Would the lady from Ile-Oluji who is so passionate about her Nigerian-ness have been spared if she was in Maiduguri and the protesters had identified her as a Christian?

Ours is one nation where the action of a stupid, drunken man or woman defecating near a church or a mosque in some remote part of the country could mean that death sentences had been passed on ethnic or religious affiliates residing somewhere else. Since the return of democracy in 1999 thousands of Nigerians have been killed through the pre-meditated actions of others. Had President Olusegun Obasanjo not acted with utmost restraint in the early days of his presidency, the storm of *Sharia* which spread through the states of the North could also have blown the regions of the South out of the

Nigerian federation. The timing of Sharia, many in The South rightly or wrongly believed, was intended to undermine his leadership. Ours is one delicate and fragile nation where a lot of homework needs to be done in order to ensure that our people can take harmonious co-existence of differences for granted.

Of course there may be whispers in some quarters that the Yoruba have demonstrated consistently over the years that members of different religions, be it Christianity or Islam, can co-exist peacefully and even celebrate religious occasions together. This "Yoruba model" may not be quite feasible in some parts of the Nigerian federation but, at least, it is important for religionists to know that a merciful god or Allah has not mandated anyone to commit murder on his behalf. While parents, religious leaders and educationalists must continue to impart the ethics of tolerance and good neighbourliness on those under their influences, it is the responsibility of the law of the land to bring its full weight to bear on anyone, no matter how highly placed, who deliberately sets out to destroy life or property belonging to others. The bitter truth is that there are Nigeria ns today who hate Nigeria so passionately, simply because they have had experiences which most of us have been lucky not to have had. They once loved Nigeria and would not have wanted to be identified as belonging to any section or group.

Nigeria will never achieve full integration. In fact many nations of the world never will. Furthermore the Nigerian situation is compounded by the facts of different languages, different cultures, contrasting and competing religions, super-imposed on regions demarcated by ethnic boundaries. However, the Nigerian nation can still be held together as a federal nation where differences co-exist peacefully. Acknowledging the realities of ethnic and religious divisions, rather than indulge in shouting slogans like those leaders of the former Soviet Union, is itself the beginning of wisdom in constitution making and political engineering. "Dictatorship of the proletariat" was one historical fallacy that crumbled under the full weight of ethnicity!

*The Guardian*

# Transforming The Semi Democratic State

The semi-democratic state, in my own definition, is a state which upholds democracy as an idea but falls short in the application of its principles. The principles of freedom of speech and association, free and fair elections as well as transparency in government constitute essential attributes of the democratic state.

Most African states, including Nigeria, fall into the category of the semi-democratic state. We have witnessed in recent months two national elections on the African continent which attracted the attention of the international community. The Kenyan election of December 2007 resulted in violent protests in which more than a thousand people were reportedly killed, while Robert Mugabe's tactics or attempts to rig the Zimbabwean presidential elections of March 2008 have kept the rest of the world waiting.

Mr Mugabe is 84; even when he was no longer popular he relied on the coercive institutions of state to sustain his rule. One characteristic of the semi-democratic state is the role undemocratic institutions such as the military and police are made to play in the democratic process. They aid and abet the rigging of elections, and are more than willing agents in the suppression of dissent. Mr Mugabe used the coercive institutions of state to devastating effect; Condaleeza Rice, the American Secretary of State described Mugabe as a "disgrace to Africa". What a "befitting" epithet to the political career of a leader who would not leave office when the ovation was loudest!

The type of electoral misbehaviour recently highlighted in Kenya and Mugabe's Zimbabwe are common place in Africa and have more or less become the tradition in Nigeria since independence in 1960. Nigeria's most recent presidential election of April 2007 was not in any way less fraudulent than the chaotic Kenyan election of December. When the Nigerian electoral game was tagged "operation do or die" by the then incumbent president no one was left in any doubt as to what the intended outcome would be. General Olusegun

Obasanjo single-handedly determined his own successor in office (as Mr Vladimir Putin would later do in the semi-democratic state of Russia) in an election that was believed to have been massively rigged in order to ensure his will prevailed. That Nigerians did not take the law into their own hands like their counterparts in Kenya should not suggest the former were more civilized. Nigeria has shed more blood than most African nations since the inception of partisan politics.

The suggestion has been made, especially by some Nigerian commentators, that a bloody revolution is needed to sort thing out. Of course revolutions have played a significant role in the history of democracy, but such revolutions were directed at sources that made democracy impossible in the first place. In Europe, for instance, revolutions have resulted in the eradication of the monarchy or curtailment of its influence. The history of revolt in some African nations has been a history of one ethnic group taking up arms against another. In Nigeria, for instance, a relatively minor religious disagreement has the capacity to provoke greater resentment than the rigging of an election. This, however, is not to say that a revolt of some sort cannot lead to positive change.

The road to true democracy is continuity. Democracy has been interrupted in Nigeria on several occasions since independence in 1960, while the American political system, for instance, has endured more than two hundred years of continuity. We may today admire the sophistication of the Clintons, Obamas and McCains but the history of American presidential contest has not always been that straightforward. George Washington's elections in 1789 and 1792 were in effect uncontested. In 1800, Thomas Jefferson defeated Aaron Burr in "in an election in which no one had a majority and the election was turned over to the House of Representatives which deliberated and voted 36 times between 11 and 17 February 1801". The first time ever that a presidential candidate would go on a nationwide campaign tour was 1860 and that candidate was Stephen Douglas who lost the presidential election to Abraham Lincoln that year. A hundred years later, in 1960, came the age of television and the first ever televised presidential debate between John F Kennedy and Richard Nixon. America's presidential elections have continued to improve in transparency from the early days when the political mafia were said to have had a big say.

The citizenry and patriotic leadership must continue to emphasise the reform of the political process. Reform of the constitution and the electoral processes is essential to correcting the mistakes of the past. Those who have successfully organised the electoral overthrow of "elected dictators" must also learn not to behave like the tyrants they replaced. Mr Morgan Tsvangirai of the Movement for Democratic Change (MDC) who has persevered over the years in his campaign against the tyranny of Mr Robert Mugabe has the historic task of launching Zimbabwe on the path of true democracy and development if he becomes president. Mr Mugabe completed his own historical task many years ago – he liberated his nation from the clutches of imperialism – but greed and fear continued to propel him in office. He remains an important historical figure in Zimbabwean politics regardless.

The political party, it must be emphasised, is an important element in the democratic arena and true democrats must be tolerant of competing ideas. The political party may have been defined as an association of like-minded individuals but this is not always the case. The political party, in the Nigerian context, is an umbrellage of diverse ethnic, religious and ideological interests. The political party itself must be disciplined for it to be effective and successful in the organisation of state and society. Nigeria's People's Democratic Party (PDP) is building itself for the future; any political party that genuinely wants to complete with the PDP must begin to widen its nets now. The political party of the future must transcend the transient ambition of the individual.

The transformation of the semi-democratic state is largely about the economic and educational transformation of society itself. The African continent, in spite of its resources, is the poorest in the world. The quality of our democracy will improve considerably once the economic and educational fortunes of our people have also improved.

192

Most Africans do not read, neither do they have access to television. Pseudo-democrats who only fend for themselves are quite happy with the status quo because all they ever want is to be worshipped.

*The Guardian, 15 April 2008*

## Still On Nigerians In Diaspora

Some time in the 1960s a report appeared in an influential magazine about Nigerians who had failed to return home after a considerable number of years in overseas countries. It was a rather derogatory account, not least because such Nigerians were perceived to have stayed behind for the shame of not having accomplished the objectives that propelled their exit from Nigeria. Overstayed male Nigerians were sarcastically called "big brother" by the newly-arrived ones.

In those days a decision to travel overseas would have been for no purpose other than educational. To remain in an overseas country for more than four years would have been considered unimaginable, except if the degree programme one was pursuing called for a longer duration of time. A heroic welcome often awaited the returnee who was held in great awe by the locals. In some remote parts of the Nigerian federation, guns blazed and masquerades danced in the street to herald the arrival of the one who had just come back from the white man's land. The returnee, especially the women, could be seen wearing white hand gloves even in the scorching Nigerian sun. Or, how else could this "been to" have been distinguished from the locals? Someone I knew returned from Great Britain in the early 1960s after a mere four year sojourn and some elders in the community were wondering if he could still eat the Nigerian food or speak the local language!

The overseas returnee, armed with a diploma of some sort, had no problem other than what choice to make between competing job opportunities. Even until about 1982 officials of the Nigerian Public Service Commission visited overseas countries on a mission to recruit university graduates for various jobs at home. It was one "age long" tradition which was discontinued once the jobs dried out and the Nigerian nation itself was on the brink of bankruptcy.

Most Nigerians were more than anxious to return home on the completion of their studies. The Nigerian Civil War of 1967-70 played some part in the new culture of Nigerians cultivating foreign countries as their homes. There were those who chose to stay out of Nigeria because the Civil War had implanted some bitterness in them. However, worsening economic conditions which began in the 1980s accounted for an unprecedented exodus of Nigerians into Europe and America. The assumption that overseas is the best place to make it was further fuelled by the free-fall of the Nigerian currency. The general poverty at home and dependency on relations abroad was such that a ninety year old father once advised a son he had not seen for ten years not to rush into coming home.

Unlike in the past when those who stayed behind were considered as failures, "diasporean" Nigerians of today are skilful professionals contributing substantially to the sustenance of their host of new nations' economy and social infrastructures. Even those who do not possess special skills perform an equally important and complimentary role in society. Nigerians in diaspora can be classified into two. The first are Nigerians who were born in Nigeria and still see Nigeria as their home, while the second group of Nigerians in diaspora are the children born in the various host nations. The latter constitutes the "diaspora proper" and the prospect of their future "repatriation" to Nigeria can only be imagined or speculated about.

Relationships between Nigeria and Nigerians in diaspora can be of mutual benefit. Acquired skills from developed overseas countries can help transform Nigeria into a developed African nation. The opportunity to be able to compare one's nation with another is an opportunity that could hardly be gained if one had not been exposed to somewhere else. The views we express on how to move Nigeria forward are honest views which should not be dismissed out of hand. Such views should be cultivated because the ambition of every patriotic Nigerian, no matter where he or she is, is for Nigeria to be the best in the world.

I have been a writer of opinion for quite a quarter of a century so I should be granted the indulgence of knowing what I am talking about. Were the Nigerian leadership to be a bit more purposeful and its members less contemptuous of journalists and the intelligentsia there have been ideas suggested in the past which should have warranted someone seeking further explanation. One is aware of the workings of government in America and Europe where those in positions of authority do not let go any idea that is considered beneficial to society. The author of an idea would not have to be the son or daughter of "former this" or "former that" before the idea is considered or implemented. We only pay lip service to the acquired skills of our nationals in Nigeria or outside. The one comment of monotonous regularity one often gets from frustrated Nigerians is that "those in government know what you are saying is right but they won't just do it". How can society make progress when the general assumption is that the leadership is only interested in what can confer immediate economic benefits on its members and their families?

*The Guardian* editorial of 2 August, highlighted the basic needs that entice every human being to an environment. Such needs include security of life and property, electricity and water, employment opportunities, health facilities and safe transportation system. The editorial was spot on in concluding that the more one is exposed to societies where these opportunities or facilities are provided in good quality and even taken for granted, the more one resents the crudity of another environment. The current Nigerian government and future ones must reflect on that competent editorial because Nigeria is one nation that needs rebuilding from the foundation.

Societal poverty makes Nigerians at home assume that their kinsmen who reside abroad are privileged. There can be no greater privilege than doing things which directly or indirectly affect one's own society and its peoples. The toilet attendant who is doing an honest job is not less privileged than the doctor or lawyer in the eyes of posterity. There would be no need for the Nigerian government to create an exclusive zone for overseas returnees who may have acquired wealth or special skills because such a gesture is both unnecessary and uncalled for and can only earn such returnees an unwanted stereotype in an ever sceptical society.

*The Guardian, 14 August 2006*

# Rough road to stability

Had Osama Bin Laden been a good student of history he probably would have thought twice before "ordering" an attack on the Twin Towers in New York on 11th September 2001. For America is that lion that resents being provoked by the dog. Ask the Japanese what they got for their attack on Pearl Harbour in December 1941; Hiroshima and Nagasaki became reference points for the damage nuclear weapons could do to humanity when America retaliated in August 1945. America hardly forgives any assaults on its people and its interests, otherwise being the most powerful nation on earth serves no useful purpose.

Talking of the "power game", my good friend Kenneth Edokpayi was a master in that subject. Kenneth had resigned his commission in the Nigerian Army to take a degree in political science at Howard University and he was quite an outstanding scholar. Kenneth would argue admirably about how superpowers coerced other nations – the fact that America could invade a nation if it badly needed oil and had been denied its supply; he could not have been wrong.

America is one former colony of Britain whose founding fathers conceived the idea of a great society. The country constituted a mere 13 independent colonies when it transformed from a confederacy to a federal nation in 1787. By a deliberate policy of expansionism, America is today a nation consisting of 50 autonomous states. This means that 37 of the current states were not original members of the Union. America has a policy of attracting other nationals to boost its population. Many continue to scramble for the American Lottery Visa.

The destination of my article is Nigeria and one makes bold to ask why the fact of our nation being an amalgam of different nationalities has continued to constitute a headache. Amalgamation, as the case of America has proved, can be a source of strength and various advantages. Even as disjointed as contemporary Nigeria is, there are still those in the African continent who look to us for leadership and inspiration. Being Nigerian quite often elicits the type of excitement seemingly reserved for the one who has been introduced as American. There is always this follow-up question, "which state or region are you from?"

The advantages of size, vibrant population and economic resources are ingredients of power and importance in the world we belong to. A prominent African writer and scholar, Cameron Duodu, once wrote in an influential magazine that it would be a major setback for Africa and the black race if Nigeria were to disintegrate. He is right, because only a nation that has more than enough space for its own people can be called the land of opportunity. It can only be out of sheer short sightedness that anyone would want the flag of his or her locality to replace that of Nigeria at the United Nations.

It is true that our nation has been visited by many avoidable tensions. The recent post-election violence claiming the lives of innocent men and women is deplorable. One feels extremely saddened because it is a primitive act which recurs shamelessly and tends to dispute the Unitarian argument. However, the leadership must not pretend that there are no serious issues to content with. Our peoples need to be educated and empowered economically for ignorance and poverty constitute great threats to peaceful co-existence. The leadership must end our prevailing culture of greed, graft and corruption and concentrate on developing our nation and our peoples.

While policies which seek to achieve egalitarianism may take years to yield positive dividends there is, however, the most urgent task of keeping fragile Nigeria together. One prays to be alive, even if only until the morning of 1 January 2016 and to be in a position to deride those who had predicted that Nigeria would disintegrate by 2015, "why is it that your prediction has failed?" What many Nigerians at home may not know is that our downfall will be celebrated by our racial detractors because they resent the projections they have about our possibilities or potential.

Of course we must plot to defeat their prediction of doom because they are quite capable of achieving their objective. The leadership question must be realistically resolved because it has proved with embarrassing consistency to be the Achilles Heel of our nation. The

Civil War of 1967-1970, the Gideon Orkar attempted coup of April 22, 1990, the June 12, 1993 annulment crisis, and the recent post-election violence, continue to warn us of the most acrimonious issue in our polity. If rotating the presidency between regions is what would bring peace and stability, so be it.

There is too much of "for instance in America" and "for instance in Britain", in our discussions, even when common sense calls for pragmatic appraisal of an issue. We must seek to understand the history and nature of these great nations in making our references. About 150 years ago, one Barack Obama, "the great orator", would have had his lips padlocked in an American sugar cane plantation, so he could not complain or eat without permission. A candidate for election – a member of the Democratic Party – once said he did not welcome a black person's vote because it would only tarnish his mandate. There was also a time in British history when probably more than half of those who voted in the Nigerian 2011 election would have been considered unfit or not rational enough to decide on how they were to be represented in the governing process. Education and ownership of property determined who got the vote; it took quite a while for women to earn the right to vote. What one is trying to emphasise here is that every nation has got a history to contend with. It is a question of whether or not one nation can learn from its own history..

Now back to the "power game", don't you think representations would have been made to pacify Osama Bin Laden if it was not America, but some tiny nation that his men had attacked? Such a tiny nation would have protested endlessly and in vain. Methinks Osama has worked positively for Obama's second term bid because his constituency now acknowledges him as a decisive leader and the Commander-in-Chief they deserve. America adulates a political leader that can competently represent their interests, both in peace and at war.

*The Guardian, 10 May 2011*

# Rough Road to Democracy

Most people in the relatively stable democratic nations of the world would find it rather difficult to understand why democracy should be causing so much pain in the so-called third world nations. The assassination of Benazir Bhutto in December 2007 and the consequent turmoil of Pakistan followed by the killings of hundreds of citizens in Kenya in the aftermath of allegedly rigged presidential elections, further reminded peoples of the peaceful democratic nations that what they now take for granted in their own nations never comes on a platter of gold.

The United States of America gained its independence from Britain in 1776. However, the Americans had to fight a system which made them pay tax without being represented in parliament. "No taxation without representation" was the memorable slogan of their war and their declaration which must guide democracy anywhere in the world is the assertion that "all men and women are created equal". The determination to give effect to that important declaration would later lead to constitutionalists to prohibit the American citizen from bearing a title of nobility. The now problematic gun culture – the right of the American citizen to have a gun- was also intended to achieve that end.

However, America is still democratising because the assertion of equality of all men and women excluded blacks for the great part of the nation's history. The history of de jure acceptance of blacks as equal to whites is only about fifty years old, coming into effect with the Civil Rights legislation of the 1960s, while de facto acceptance of equality is still evolving. However, things are looking good because substantial progress has been made.

Neither can Great Britain claim to have perfected its democracy. The nature and extent of privileges enjoyed by the Monarchy is an on-going debate. The history of democracy in Britain has been a history of the ordinary citizen challenging the Crown and the so-called royal prerogative. It is also a history of organised challenge to the assumptions of the aristocracy. The British Monarch is now a mere constitutional one – courtesy of the revolt led by Oliver Cromwell in the 17th century – while many other European countries including France, Germany and Russia got rid of theirs in violent revolutions. The emergence of a controversial King or Queen could spell the end of the monarchy in Britain.

Be that as it may, democracy and its institutions crept in gradually. The right to vote did not come to many on a platter of gold. Requirements of property and education meant many were excluded from the democratic process. Voting rights did not come to women until quite recently. We may now refer to some societies as civilised not least because their citizens readily comply to rules and regulations but such civility did not come about easily. In Britain, for instance, there was once a time when a relatively minor offence attracted severe punishment. Convicts were ex-communicated and distant Australia became more or less Britain's prison for such convicts.

The universal definition of democracy is that provided by the great Abraham Lincoln as "the government of the people, for the people, and by the people". Democracy is not just an approach to political governance but a culture which touches on every facet of human life. The major problem of democracy in some societies is that it is a new value system in competition with already established structure which are at best contradictory. The authoritarian feudal structures of some societies derive their authenticity from tradition and religion. Until the contradictions of state and society have been resolved, our democracy will be a mere imitation of what obtains somewhere else.

In Nigeria, for instance, the traditional system co-exists with the modern democratic system. There is nothing like the King or Queen of Nigeria but traditional rulers exist as heads of cities, towns and villages. The British approached political governance in Nigeria through a system of indirect rule, making use of the Chiefs. The politician seeking political power wants to be in the good books of the traditional ruler and some might want to parade a chieftaincy title of some sort. Traditional rulers are among the most affluent in Nigerian society; those in big cities receive multiple salaries from local government councils in their areas of jurisdiction. It is hard to envisage a revolution that would end Nigeria's traditional institutions.

The electoral democracy into which we were introduced has been characterised by failure. The rigging culture has become our electoral culture. The recent events in Kenya are also an indication that election rigging is an African disease. The typical African leader does not believe in leaving office voluntarily or in being defeated in the process of re-election. If the Constitution stipulates two terms, the typical African leader interprets it to mean a minimum of two terms in office. Mr Kwai Kibaki of Kenya is a most recent example, while Robert Mugabe of Zimbabwe has been one long term misleader in that respect. The United States of America has been governed by one constitution since 1787, while Britain is not even guided by a written one; the typical African leader believes the Constitution could be changed at every conceivable opportunity, to suit his whims and caprices.

Is there a future for democracy in Africa? One likes to be optimistic and therefore say there is. One's optimism derives from the belief that education can play a big part in the future of democracy in our continent. Most of the current crop of African leaders (or rulers) belong to the first generation of educated men and women in their respective families, while the percentage of the educated in society itself is generally low. True democracy belongs to the future when a more assertive, refined and rational citizenry dominates the political space. With successive generations of educated men and women the outlook on life will be a lot different from what it currently is. A country like Britain can boast of more than a thousand years of education; the University of Oxford is more than 900 years old while Nigeria's oldest university, the University of Ibadan will be 60 this year. The point one is trying to make here is that ours is still a very young nation.

Future economic outlook will also bolster democracy. The current generation knows no other route to wealth and fame other than politics but that should change when economic opportunities widen. Look at Al Gore and the name he has made for himself on the issue of Climate Change, which is to say a man or woman of stature can find relevance outside partisan politics. When corrupt politicians retire to nowhere other than prison, those who seek wealth will know where to go. The Press and Judiciary in Nigeria are doing a good job but the people themselves must feel democratic for democracy to be the culture they so much crave.

*The Guardian, 15 January 2008*

## 'Education, education, education'

It was reported in several Nigerian newspapers that Pastor Enoch Adejare Adeboye, General Overseer of the Redeemed Christian Church of God, endowed a professional chair in Mathematics at the University of Nigeria, Nsukka. The highly esteemed religious leader was reported to have, in the past, also made similar endowments to the universities of Ibadan and Lagos. This thoughtful contribution of his deserves commendation, as do the contributions of others in the all-important area of education.

The need and demand for education will know no bounds. Tony Blair, erstwhile Prime Minister of Great Britain, talked emphatically of 'Education, education, education' while unveiling the priorities of the Labour government in 2007. If education still enjoys pride of place in a nation that has had education for more than a thousand years, it simply means it cannot be any less in a developing nation such as ours. Education provides the key to development; any nation that genuinely seeks development and an end to ignorance must begin with the education of its citizens. Education is the route to achieving the much-desired unity that has eluded our nation for many decades.

The colonial masters sowed the seeds of disunity in Nigeria when they chose an opportunistic approach to education. If Western education had been emphasised in the North as it was in the South, Nigerians might have had a better understanding of themselves today. However, it serves no useful purpose blaming the colonial masters whose priority might have been exploitation rather than development; the blame is with post-independence Nigerian governments which have failed woefully to redress what was an historical imbalance in spite of abundant opportunities to do so. A new generation of Nigerian leaders must now take up the challenge and redirect the course of history to the benefit of all. The Goodluck Jonathan administration must make education its priority. This same clarion call goes to the various state governments and Local Government Councils. They must fund education as well as develop educational policies that help, in the long run, to achieve the objectives of development and a balanced federation. Our education must be geared towards reducing religious bigotry; it is in doing this that the future of Nigeria can be secured. The Goodluck Jonathan administration must direct its focus to the North. One does not seek to patronise or insult by making this suggestion; on the contrary, the suggestion arises from one's aspiration for a truly united and purposeful Nigerian nation. The Jonathan administration would need to admonish religious and political leaders of the need to reduce the problems posed by lopsided education and poverty, even if the latter is a national scourge of embarrassing proportions.

The truth of the matter, forget about their corruption, is that the no government is rich enough to fulfil all the educational aspirations of its people. The privileged among us must contribute their quota in making education available to all. Those who have benefitted from education and are now comfortable must remember to 'plough back' into society and their former institutions. This has been one culture that keeps the great educational institutions of Europe and America at the very top. The culture of wanting to make our former schools, colleges and universities better than when we left them, must be embraced by all.

The example of Pastor Adejare Adeboye is worth celebrating as well as emulating. We must use our wealth to promote education and the unity of Nigeria. The unity of Nigeria is important, even viewed from a selfish point of view. A proprietor whose newspaper is selling 250,000 copies a day may have to make do with less that 5,000 if that locality of his or hers were to become an independent nation! Our future is enhanced or diminished by what becomes of Nigeria.

Our nation boasts the richest African in the person of Alhaji Aliko Dangote. The message to Dangote is that there is a world of difference between being famous and being great. 'Fame' is a temporary phenomenon while 'greatness' is enduring. A Dangote Foundation, if one does not already exist, could do for Nigeria what the Ford Foundation has been doing beyond the boarders of the

United States of America. The famous businessman can use his colossal wealth to take the education revolution to the North of Nigeria in particular, and the whole of Nigeria generally. Mr Dangote and our men and women of financial means can write their names in gold by seizing upon the moment of history.

Nigerians are generally kind and generous. The late Chief Gani Fawehinmi awarded many scholarships to Nigerians irrespective of their ethnic and religious origins. The late Chief MKO Abiola once gave a million naira – a colossal sum in those days – to each of the then existing universities. Chief Wole Olanipekun has been making a difference in the lives of the younger generation in Ekiti State. There are numerous others, not known to this writer who are doing their own bit for prosperity. However, what one is advocating for the mega rich is an endowment of a lasting span and impact such as the Rhodes Scholarship established at the University of Oxford in 1902 and the Ford Foundation established in 1936.

Of course, we can all play our part in the crusade to make our society one of educated men and women. Education is a continuing process, even for the educated elite. Every village, town and city deserves to have a functioning public library. There should be no excuse for a truly educated individual not to be able to read a newspaper on a daily basis. The Local Government Councils have a duty to establish public libraries, while public spirited men and women can continue to sustain such libraries with various donations that include books. Our pensioners can relive their working lives by helping their communities in voluntary capacities. We do not all have to be 'His or Her Excellencies' to drive Nigeria forward.

*The Guardian, 24 June 2011*

# The presidency in 2015

ONE concept I tried to clarify in the run-up to the presidential election of 2011 was that of "re-election". I argued then that President Goodluck Jonathan could not have been seeking re-election because he was only a vice-presidential candidate to the one elected president in 2007. One can only be deemed to be seeking re-election to a position one had been elected to in the first place. The clarification I was attempting to make may have become clearer now that the political future of President Jonathan has been enjoying some debate in academic and political circles (see, for instance, Chidi Amuta, "Jonathan and 2015", This Day Newspaper, 3rd April 2012).

Dr. Amuta, in the useful article referred to above, opined that the constitution of the Federal Republic of Nigeria, as well as the cause of democracy would be strengthened if Goodluck Jonathan were not denied the constitutional right to seek re-election in 2015. He was not saying that the Peoples Democratic Party (PDP) must present Jonathan as its flag bearer, even if his lacklustre performance had continued into the future. What Chidi Amuta seems to be anticipating, just like the rest of us, is the controversy the PDP "zoning" policy of alternating the presidency between the North and the South could engender in the very near future. There would be those reminding Goodluck Jonathan that his tenure had expired, not least because the argument once conjured in favour of his candidacy was that he was continuing with the mandate he jointly held with the late President Umaru Musa Yar'Adua. His supporters said the mandate was inseparable, but would their argument still hold in 2015?

Of course, President Goodluck Jonathan can seek re-election in 2015 – if dictates of selfish interest prevail. The fact that he had been sworn into office twice would not have meant he had served a second term in office. One recalls the case of Lyndon B Johnson whose ascension to the American presidency compares with Jonathan's route to office. Johnson had succeeded the assassinated John F. Kennedy in 1963, won an election of his own in 1964 and would have sought re-election in 1968, but for the fact that he had become very unpopular because of the negative outcome of America's conflict in Vietnam. Not constitutionally barred, he took the decent route of withdrawing from seeking his party's nomination.

Goodluck Jonathan is not unaware of the possible crisis his wanting to continue in office beyond 2015 could generate. His declaration of an intention not to seek re-election in 2015 may not be unconnected with this. However, a promise made out of desperation or expediency may not always hold, not least because what we are talking about here is power and its alluring influences. The President had warned his ministers and assistants against unguarded statements about 2015; however, he could be the very one encouraging them to sing his praises and sound public opinion in the not too distant future. The PDP is in for a major crisis, but can the so-called opposition parties benefit from this? Amuta explored this question in his excellent article.

The opinion here is that the very reasons the PDP may run into crisis in 2015 also explains why the opposition parties might not be able to take advantage of their situation. The so-called "progressives" have a disappointing history as they have been unable to progress beyond the confines of ethnic boundaries. Regional sentiments have been the dominating influence in all of this. There are all sorts of progressives in the various regions. The regional element in our democracy must be addressed in an improved constitution if we were to have a national progressive party. Being myopically pre-occupied with a political arrangement that has worked elsewhere may not have helped the cause of our democracy.

I say it is futile to be preoccupied with political arrangements that have worked elsewhere because what we have not been able to photocopy are the cultural elements that sustain them in the host nations. In Britain, for instance, the institution of the monarchy has provided stability to the parliamentary system of government, which originated from that great nation. What we celebrate in Nigeria is exactly what truly – republican America rejects – privileges arising from the circumstances of birth. It is clearly stated in their constitution that "no American citizen shall bear a title of nobility". Here in Nigeria, politicians envy traditional rulers for the unsolicited respect they command, while the latter also envy the former for the monies they are able to steal!

I should be suggesting to those with the powers to review or amend the national constitution that rotational presidency is most appropriate for Nigeria. Zoning the presidency could be the most assured way of inducing competitive political parties and ideologies to traverse the various divides. In a society that is as divided as ours, it could also be the most assured way objectively, of fishing out our political leaders, based on merit, rather than primordial affiliations. Zoning could be our own contribution to the principle of federalism, which, more than anything else, emphasises equality and fairness in the relationship of participating units. Democracy itself should be about peace and stability in one's own nation.

*The Guardian,11 April 2012*

# Still on rotational presidency

We do not do not have a "rotational presidency" yet, what we do have is "zoning" by individual political parties. Once there is a rotational presidency, the rules guiding the principle will be elegantly stated in the national constitution with all political parties mandated to follow them.

This writer has been one long-term advocate of the idea of a rotational presidency, not least because of the belief that it provides one effective way of cross-cutting the cleavages of ethnicity and religion. A situation whereby two or more political parties pick their candidates from a particular region of the federation tends to induce intra-ethnic competition and national voting based on the perception of candidates and the political parties they represent. The 1999 election that pitched General Olusegun Obasanjo against Chief Olu Falae, both Yoruba, provides one example. General Obasanjo was not the popular choice of the Yoruba but nevertheless won that election. It was one contest in which ethnicity and religion had no place in the consideration of voters.

Dr Reuben Abati did a commendable critique of the so-called core - north in a recent article, "Rotational Presidency And The Core North?" published in The Guardian of April 18, 2010. It is about the assumption of, or claim to, superiority or pre-eminence by one sub-regional group over and above others, The basic and incontrovertible tenet of democracy anywhere in the world is the acceptance of equality by all men and women. The good thing about rotational presidency as revealed by the contest between Chief Olu Falae and General Olusegun Obasanjo is that the way candidates are perceived in the national constituency is more important than what they are in their narrow constituency. A candidate from a so-called periphery of a geo-political zone cannot be disadvantaged in this regard.

This writer has attempted to illustrate in his first book, The Search for a Nigerian Political System (London, 1986) that there is more to rotational presidency than the "turn by turn" thing assumed by cynics.

There is a sense in which such a system could help us in making the most rational decision in the context of our nation's realities as there are competent individuals in all regions of the federation. It is both presumptuous and insulting to say that rotational presidency encourages mediocrity.

With nothing separating our political parties other than the ambition of migrant politicians, it can only be assumed that someone seeking to be president for the first time would be competent. Even then, the quality of the electorate making the all-important political decision cannot be ignored It is in this latter sphere of our political endeavour that we are still many miles away from where we think we are. The qualifications that help independent voting culture are in short supply Poverty and illiteracy compete with embarrassing determination.

One is not comfortable with the notion or assumption that rotational presidency is "undemocratic". Structures of democracy cannot be separated from a nation's needs for peace and stability. In short, there is no unique, universal model of democracy. Chiefs Ebenezer Babatope and John Oyegun, two intelligent and mature minds in matters of our political history and behaviour, emphasized the realities that make rotational presidency so attractive in their interviews with The Guardian published on April 18, 2010. It serves no useful purpose being sentimental or emotional in matters of this nature. Being once a colonized people should not mean we cannot de-colonize our minds to be able to accept that the political arrangements of other nations could not have been meant for us.

Great Britain is undoubtedly one of the oldest and most accomplished democratic nations of the world, yet the British Head of State is a hereditary monarch and the Prime Minister can only be someone who is both a Member of Parliament and Leader of the political party with the majority of seats in the legislature. The monarch "appoints" the Prime Minster, a tradition which began in 1721 when King George I, who was said to be unable to speak English, appointed Robert Walpole as "Leader of the Commons". The Prime Minister seeks the permission or authorization of the monarch before he or she can call

211

for a general election. It will take a lot of dreaming for anyone outside the royal lineage to be King or Queen in Britain, as it will also require a lot of patience or waiting for the elected politician to be Prime Minister!

Neither is the United States of America an "unreasonable" democratic nation, because the founding fathers ensured equality among states, irrespective of their size or population, by creating a bi-camera legislature. However, the nation's electoral college system means a candidate with the highest number of popular votes may still not win the presidency; a few large states could determine the outcome of a presidential election.

One feels amused when some Nigerians race into talking about how Barack Obama, the Orator, has become President of the United States of America and seek immediate replication of this magic in Nigeria. They do not seem to remember that there was once a time when the black person in America had his or her mouth padlocked so that he or she could only eat, drink or speak when the owner permitted it. Nigeria has the makings of a great nation; it is our collective responsibility to fight the injustices bred by corruption and other societal ills that constitute an impediment to that greatness! Improvements in the educational and economic well-being of our peoples, violently frustrated by the corruption of the elite, are the prerequisites of appropriate behaviour that helps the cause of democracy and unity.

Rotational presidency may not be as great as using the computer to determine who should be leader, it is nevertheless both necessary and desirable in the context of our nation. This writer has argued consistently that the workability of leadership's rotation can only be guaranteed within the framework of a single-term, not least because it is both unreasonable and problematic to hold two consecutive elections in order to elect a candidate from a particular region of the federation. The implications of this absurdity have been highlighted elsewhere by this writer. Suffice it to say that the campaign for "zoning" to be constitutionalised into "rotation" continues here, knowing fully well that those who seek to be perpetual presidential candidates may not support it!!

Rotational presidency, if included in the constitution as contemporary realities suggest it should, it may not be a permanent feature no matter how lofty an idea we think it is. It is customary practice in democratic nations with written constitutions to periodically review and possibly amend any provision of the constitution only when it may be deemed to have served its purpose. The idea of a rotational presidency cannot be an exemption. There is no doubt that a future generation will have its say in all of this, ridicule us if they so desire, but the duty we owe that future is to save the present.

*The Guardian,22 April 2010*

# Nigeria can be great

MY gradual re-integration into Nigerian society, after so many years in overseas countries came a bit sooner than scheduled. I had penciled in my diary a must visit to Nigeria about October or November but then came a birthday present of a travel ticket from my wife. I thought about changing the dates fixed in the ticket, principally because they clashed with two major sporting events of great interest, Wimbledon Tennis and the 2006 World Cup finals. Wimbledon , in particular, is one annual sporting event I look forward to with excitement and the Nigerian television does not have a history of covering it.

However, I chose an early visit to Nigeria over and above my passion for sports. With the many unpredictabilities of life, an opportunity to be re-united with members of one's family is something that should not be procrastinated about. A recent home video which featured a relatively younger childhood friend smiling with virtually half of his teeth gone, further warned me that the ageing process could be wicked!

For anyone who has traveled in and out of Nigeria a few times, an encounter with officials of the Nigerian airport is always in mind. The last time I visited Nigeria I witnessed an interesting encounter between a customs official and a Nigerian who had tried to impress by saying his brother was the supreme boss of the Murtala Muhammed Airport . The customs official who was after nothing but a bribe, asked the Nigerian what was in his hand luggage. On being told it was ground rice, the customs official said "you think you are smart, the Babangida government has placed a ban on the importation of rice but you went to grind your own". He got a few naira before the young man was allowed to go.

When I arrived at the Nigerian airport recently one superficial impression was that extortionist tendencies had become something of the past. However, it was one impression which did not last very long because when I was returning to Britain three weeks later I saw one visibly disturbed woman haggling over a "fee" with a customs official. She probably had an item in her luggage which required a small bribe before its passage could be guaranteed. This not withstanding, the general airport environment appeared better sanitised and contemporary officials looked more professional and discrete.

Nigeria is a beautiful country inhabited by the warmest and most exciting human beings on earth but one nevertheless wonders why its political authorities assume it is the environment for tourists and investors. The tourist, in particular, looks forward to a comfortable and safe transportation system which, on the evidence of what is available in Lagos, Nigeria does not offer.

The smart tourist wants to be able to pick out a small book or pamphlet in an overseas embassy or at the airport which provides information on the travel and accommodation in the nation he or she is visiting. Signs and directions provided along the roads tend to guide the sophisticated tourist who prefers to discover things with minimum enquiring. Rather than providing this information or directions, bill boards along inter-city roads are pasted with posters of those wanting to be governors or senators in 2007.

The Nigerian transportation system is chaotic, with vehicles which should long have been consigned to scrap yards or improvised as silos for the storage of farm products, picking and dropping off passengers without regard for designated bus stops even in the important city of Lagos . The foreign officials who would recommend Nigeria for tourism can only have come from comparatively backward countries

I was a critic of Okada, not least because I believe motor cycles are not commercial vehicles. On visiting Nigeria I saw Okada in action. With the picture of this menacing "business" permanently fixed in my memory the authorities which made its existence and triumph possible do not have a place for decency in their hearts. Crude and dangerous, Okada may have come to stay because the various Nigerian governments have no clue about the problem of transportation or unemployment

Public transport in a modern society cannot be a free-for-all business. The modern Nigerian society of my dream is one in which the transport system is handled by registered companies, with government providing guidelines for the comfort and safety of passengers. Such companies which welcome all interested men and women as shareholders become partners with governments in the development and maintenance of roads by virtue of the enormous taxes accruing from their profits. With oil money the talent to generate wealth from other sectors of the economy may have gone.

An uninterrupted supply of electricity and water should by now be taken for granted in the Nigerian society. Nigeria 's epileptic supply of electricity, in particular, is a major headache for most homes. Ordinary Nigerians have come to accept that electricity is one luxury which can come when it likes, while the middle class which has become indulged in its magic expends substantial portions of its income on generating electricity. The popular saying in Nigeria is that the generator provides electricity, while PHCN (the electricity providing authority) stands by in case of failure.

The one thing the Nigerian authorities should now know is that the nation's supply of electricity cannot be monopolised by a single body. In a nation as big and populous as Nigeria , the supply of electricity should be decentralised along regions or even states. Experiences in Europe and America suggest that the private sector is more competent in this regard, as the business of electricity and water supply is open to competition.

If anything, Nigeria is arguably the most political nation in the entire world. Nigeria is that important African nation where politics holds sway over political governance and development. Politics is a thriving business, a market where both the unemployed and the rich scramble for fortune and more fortune.

216

There was a programme on television in which one political analyst assumed that the best way to improve the quality of legislation and political governance in Nigeria was to impose varied educational qualifications on different categories of elective offices. I do not quite share that viewpoint. The one viewpoint I do share is that the quality of political governance is a reflection of the quality of the political environment itself. The larger Nigerian society that is able to define its rights, aspirations and priorities will get a better deal from those that govern them. Theirs is one sphere in which the activities of political interest groups can be very important in a democracy.

Nigeria can be a great nation because the attributes of human and material resources are there in abundance. There has been much talk about the economic reforms of the Olusegun Obasanjo administration but one hopes that this "rhetoric" can translate into visible improvements in the quality of our people's lives.

While discussions with some informed Nigerians like Professor Ladipo Adamolekun, Dr Reuben Abati and Chief Wole Olanipekun (SAN) offer useful insight into current Nigerian political environment, my gratitude for three weeks of free accommodation and free meals, must go to Dr Ayo Teriba, his lovely wife Yinka and those well-behaved children of theirs who fondly called me "Daddy Oxford". If the Teribas had not got a generator to get the television working I might still not believe that Italy won the World Cup! The saying that "seeing is believing" makes the acclaimed resurrection of Jesus Christ a matter for serious dispute in the court of non-believers.

*The Guardian, 25 July 2006*

# PART 11

# THE 2015 PRESIDENTIAL ELECTION

## SYNOPSIS

*The most important democratic event following the first publication of this book in 2013, was the 2015 presidential election. The following articles have therefore been added as an update to my thoughts and commentaries.*

*The 2015 election, more than any election before it, attracted the attention of the international community as well as Nigerians themselves with unequal passion. The international community feared for its outcome, not least because of a history of post-election violence. President Barack Obama of the United States of America, among many world statesmen, pleaded for a peaceful election. The prospect of a disorganised Nigerian estate, both to its immediate neighbours and the world community at large, could hardly be contemplated.*

*Nigerians themselves feared the worst. The fear of a possible disintegration of their nation was not helped by threats of violence being made here and there should the outcome of the election favour one group against another. With the Boko Haram insurgency in the North-East geo-political zone raging with election preparations, such fear was credible.*

*However, the outcome of the election defied widely held fears. Both Professor Attahiru Jega, Chairman of the Independent National Electoral Commission (INEC) and President Goodluck Jonathan, were lavishly praised for different reasons. The former and his team for conducting a relatively successful election, while Jonathan was praised for sportsmanship in conceding victory to his victorious challenger, retired General Muhammadu Buhari.*

*With the 2015 election concluded, attention must focus on what can be taken from it as the reform of the processes of democracy must continue. A "post-mortem" exercise, as a matter of fact, must follow every election, not the least in a nation whose democracy is still at the rudimentary stage.*

*The first observation in the Nigerian 2015 election is the role money played in its politics. We seem to be operating an electoral democracy meant for the rich, or those who can risk becoming debtors in pursuit of their ambitions. The amounts of money stipulated for "tickets" into the various elective offices are outrageous. Many honest Nigerians can hardly partake in elections because of this.*

*Equally outrageous is the assumption that there is a monetary tag on every prospective Nigerian voter. There is hardly any doubt that it could be expensive to get political messages across via the media in general but the assumption that money or monetary gifts must be distributed to Nigerian voters is highly insulting and should be criminalised, both for the giver as well as for the taker. The sheering news from the 2015 election may have been the disappointment by those who still failed to win their elections despite having spent so much attempting to induce favourable outcomes.*

*There is also a sense in which many celebrated the defeat of President Goodluck Jonathan, candidate of the Peoples Democratic Party. Even when they did not belong to any of the political parties, they nevertheless felt infuriated by the volume of naira that vested interests pumped into his campaign funds. They wished for his defeat because of that, so the rich and their monumental obscenity could be shamed in a democracy that is about every Nigerian. There must be an enforceable cap on how much can be donated to individuals and political parties, as well as how much could be spent on electoral campaigns.*

*Another observation from the election is that primordial sentiments still predominate. There was ethnic, regional and religious voting in most of the geo-political zones. The outcome of the presidential election hinged on who benefitted more from the balance of sentiments. Of course, the election of General Muhammadu Buhari,candidate of the All Progressives Congress, was popular both at home and abroad; the fact of sentiments in Nigerian politics nevertheless remains intrinsic with the nature of society itself.*

*The South-South and South-East geo-political zones, for no considerations other than ethnic, voted overwhelmingly for Goodluck Jonathan, while it was unlikely the North could suddenly have turned the bastion of progressive ideology were the presidential candidate of the PDP to have come from that region and that of the rival APC from the South. The North voted overwhelmingly for Buhari, a revered member of the region.*

*Finally, there is hardly any doubt that Professor Jega and his colleagues did a competent and patriotic job. However, issues of election malpractices and election-related violence and killings must not be ignored. A future campaign based on issues, rather than personal attacks and desperation, will go a long way in educating Nigerians that democracy belongs in the pantheon of decent cultures.*

## Our Intolerant "Democrats"

The military boys have become some kind of political lepers most discriminating Nigerians would not want to touch! This, indeed, has been good for our "democracy" so far. In the not-too-distant past, the military boys would have been called upon, or invited, to expel the politicians whenever their nuisance infuriated us or them.

For instance, Nigerians would have prevailed upon the military to terminate democracy when former President Olusegun Obasanjo engaged in a "political brawl" with his deputy, Alhaji Atiku Abubakar, in the latter half of his second term in office. The process of political governance suffered, while everything was about an Obasanjo-Atiku imbroglio – something Reuben Abati tagged the "Bolekaja presidency". The quarrel, we are told, was about Obasanjo's extra-constitutional "third term agenda" clash with Atiku's "first term" ambition or aspiration.

Again, what would have been the right timing for the desperate or ambitious coup plotter came when President Umaru Yar'Adua was dying and his loyalists would want us believe he was merely holidaying! The fear that the Presidency could be shifting to another region of the federation, meant Yar'Adua would continue to be "patched up" even when it had become apparent that he was incapacitated. If it were possible, his death could have been denied! It required the intervention of the Save Nigeria Group, an ad hoc interest group, for reason to prevail and the reins of political power to be transferred to Yar'Adua's deputy, Goodluck Jonathan.

Goodluck Jonathan's Presidency, following the 2011 election especially, has been grappling with insecurity problems. The escalation of violence in the North-East geopolitical zone, the Boko Haram insurgency in particular, could have compelled the prospective coup plotter of old to get the marshal music playing. The crisis, escalated as it was in the aftermath of Jonathan's election, was believed to be politically-motivated. However, the military did not intervene and democracy struggled on.

In all of this, we must thank the regimes of Generals Ibrahim Babangida and Sani Abacha. The annulment of the presidential election of June 12 1993, during the regime of the former and the madness or tyranny in governance during that of the latter, meant politicians had earned the licence to continue to misbehave in their customary tradition. The military would appear to have been thoroughly discredited and this might have been the saving grace for the democracy of today. It became clear to all and sundry that the military boys are equally as corrupt and purposeless as the political cobwebs they once swept from the corridors of power.

However, it would be too presumptuous to assume that the current licence – a licence to loot and misbehave – cannot expire or be withdrawn. The return of the politics of intolerance, with the police and security agents seemingly compromised, portends great danger to the peace and political fortunes of Nigeria. The Rivers State crisis, where political personalities and their "spouses" have continued to engage in a show of power, could replicate the Western Region of the 1960s. The arbitrary detention of individuals even when all they did was to make "odious" but non-violent statements, runs against the prerequisite of freedom of speech as one of the basic tenets of democratic culture. Warning all and sundry about the implications of rigged elections in 2015, hardly threatens our collective peace. It could only have been those planning to rig the election who should be worried!

There are not a few who would remind Jonathan and our security agents of their seeming endorsement of "violent statements" when made by those sympathetic to the current dispensation. For instance, the threat of violence should Jonathan not be re-elected in 2015 blackmails Nigerians collectively. One would have thought our President, being one democrat, would condemn such a statement publicly. An independent and professional security apparatus could also have had cause to question those who issue threats of violence against the state and society.

There is this thing I call the "blackmailing influence of oil". The fear of militants in the oil producing region seems to have gripped the entire nation as well as compromised the sense of honesty and judgment of our leaders and elders. Jonathan himself is in a kind of dilemma. Even if he had agreed with others that he would not be seeking re-election in 2015, the fear of the militants means it is one agreement he might renege upon. He could be "disowned" by his own immediate constituency or castigated a "coward", if he were to fail to throw his political cap into the ring, which means honour and integrity could be secondary in this matter; we will wait and see.

The putative 2015 elections would hardly make a difference from previous ones. The utterances of politicians promise that customary primordial sentiments would always conspire. The series of defections we have been witnessing, especially with latter-day progressives swelling the rank and file of the All Progressives

Congress could have been about Jonathan and the rejection of his suspected ambition. A rigged or disputed 2015 election, if history were to repeat itself, could mean there would be more jobs for diggers of mass graves. A pessimistic scenario, this would seem, but not when those we have as leaders lack the talent to work towards peace and accommodation. The prediction of doom, made by foreign busybodies who very much wished the worst to happen, could have got genuinely patriotic leaders vowing that it would not happen – not just in words but in their collective deeds. There are those who have benefited from Nigeria but whose spirit somehow revolts against her.

*Punch, 29 January 2014*

# Tough Election in Prospect

It is an indisputable fact of life that we all want to be proved right when we have made predictions. The prophet who has predicted doom and gloom praises the Almighty God for his gift, even if it is a whole village that has been ravaged by fire. In a similar vein, those who have warned or predicted the possible disintegration of our nation would probably raise up their glasses in celebration if a calamity of unimaginable proportions were to befall us in 2015, the very year they have identified as the fateful year.

One is not in a position to know the discussions that take place in governmental circles, or among the privileged ones in the Council of State. Suffice to say that leaders of any serious nation would long have deliberated on the report that projects so much danger, with a view to mending delicate fences.

Most informed Nigerians know that the presidential election slated for February could be one source of danger. Prof. Bolaji Akinyemi wrote an open letter to that effect on Monday, admonishing President Goodluck Jonathan and Maj. Gen. Muhammadu Buhari (retd.), presidential candidates of our two main political parties, to do their best in preventing or curtailing possible post-election violence. Pastor Tunde Bakare had earlier warned that there might be no election in 2015, if the current state of insecurity in the country continued. Some prominent Nigerians – Anthony Cardinal Olubunmi Okogie, Chief Afe Babalola, and Prof. Ben Nwabueze, among others – have pointedly asked President Jonathan to supervise the 2015 elections, rather than participate in it, for the sake of peace in the polity.

This writer is one of ordinary Nigerians who share their view. Jonathan had himself told us in the past that he would not be seeking re-election in 2015, and it is an open secret that his party, the Peoples Democratic Party, has a formula of alternating the Presidency between the South and the North, something which was somehow truncated in order to accommodate his ambition for understandable reasons.

President Jonathan would require a lesson in the science of human behaviour if he assumed that many did not feel offended by what was to them some kind of political dishonesty. Not a few still begrudge him privately, even when they pretend to be going along with him publicly.

More significantly, the eligibility of President Jonathan to seek a further term in office is highly contestable. Should he contest the election without this matter being resolved, there would be those waiting to see if he could be sworn into office for a third time – the constitution seems to allow a maximum of two times. Should he win the 2015 election, his opponents would want to ensure that his joy did not last by taking him up on constitutional grounds.

Forget about those desperate noises being made by the so-called Transformation Ambassadors of Nigeria, Jonathan may not be the most popular president on earth seeking re-election. Telephone interviews with some of those who voted for him in 2011 reveal they might not be doing so in 2015. They claim to have been disappointed by his performance, his modest achievements having been rubbished by allegations of escalating official corruption and mediocre handling of security issues.

The reasons they adduced for supporting him in 2011 seem to no longer appeal. Regardless of whether or not Asiwaju Bola Tinubu of the defunct Action Congress of Nigeria entered into a secret arrangement to support Jonathan to the detriment of his own party, most members of his party in its Yoruba stronghold voted for Jonathan on strongly-held sentiments. They were of the opinion that the North had dominated the leadership position for too long, that a member of the minority ethnic groups in the South had previously never been elected national leader, and that Jonathan came from the region that produces the wealth of the nation.

*Daily Trust, 25 December 2014*

# Forget Re-election, Fight Boko Haram

Those comparing Goodluck Jonathan to Nelson Mandela are being dishonest. President Jonathan knows from the inner temple of his thoughts that he does not possess the strength of character that defined Mandela as one of the greatest icons in modern history.

There was a once-upon-a-time Nelson Mandela who took on the apartheid system in South Africa and paid dearly for it; he was incarcerated for 27 years. Mandela came out of prison to restate exactly the statement that earned that incarceration in the first place. He would later become the first black president of his nation. Unlike the culture of his greedy cousins and nephews in the rest of Africa, Mandela voluntarily vacated office after serving a single term of four years.

In contrast to Mandela's experiences, it has been an easy ride to political power for Jonathan. He is not known to have ever carried a placard demonstrating anywhere on behalf of Nigeria. On various occasions, he has made rather ambiguous and conflicting statements about his intentions for the future. Jonathan would have been Vice-President and President of the Federal Republic of Nigeria for eight years by May 29, 2015.

President Jonathan should be fighting the Boko Haram insurgency, not seeking a re-election in 2015. Although he inherited "BokoHaramism" from previous administrations, the phenomenon has nevertheless defined his own administration. The abduction of more than 200 schoolgirls from their Chibok hostels captured the imagination of the rest of the world. Failure to rescue those girls after more than 200 days in captivity, if one must be brutally honest, has inevitably rubbished the leadership capability of Jonathan and the efficiency of the Nigerian military.

It should be worrying that Boko Haram insurgents have acquired a substantial portion of Nigerian territory, declaring it an "Islamic Caliphate". Quite a number of Nigerians holding sensitive positions, even in the military, have become more or less like refugees! They cannot go home because their towns and villages have been taken over by the insurgents. Re-election should, in the present circumstances, be the least priority of President Jonathan, knowing full well that disputed elections could be one distraction the Boko Haram insurgents would exploit to devastating advantage.

The putative 2015 presidential election promises to be the most divisive election in the history of Nigeria. Unlike the 2011 election which pitted Jonathan against three presidential candidates from the North, the 2015 election could be one between him and a candidate of the All Progressives Congress from that region. The current tension between regions and religions suggests a most acrimonious election in prospect.

There could be a time in the life of a nation when the sacrifice and patriotism of an individual are what a nation requires to navigate a most trying period. We are facing that time in the history of our nation. The rights and privileges of a genuinely patriotic leader would take a secondary position when the national interest is at stake. The participation of Goodluck Jonathan in the 2015 election promises an outcome that could be violently contested, going by the threats from regions with perceived vested interests.

*The Guardian, 6 November 204*

# The Clog in the Ambition of Jonathan

The eligibility of President Goodluck Jonathan to seek re-election in 2015 could demand another "doctrine of necessity" for it to sail through. Of course, it could also demand a need to establish a precedent borrowing from experience elsewhere.

The hastily cobbled together Constitution of 1999 would appear not to have foreseen that a President could die while in office, or even impeached or incapacitated. However, the intention of its drafters to limit the President to a maximum of eight years in office is hardly in doubt. The 1999 Constitution recommends two terms of four years each, and stipulates that the oath of office to the coveted office of President cannot be taken more than two times—something that must be worrying for President Goodluck Jonathan who would have been president for less than six years by 2015, but has already been sworn into office twice.

The somehow spurious argument conjured in support of the future ambition of Jonathan, even by supposedly informed lawyers, is that since he was not the one elected as President in 2007, the oath of office he took in 2010 to complete what would have been the first term of the late President Umaru Yar'Adua, should not count in his favour. I counter that argument by asking if that oath of office should still not have counted had Jonathan ascended the Presidency much earlier, for it is reasonably foreseeable that a President could be dead, even immediately after he or she had been sworn into office. Moreover, the oath of office he took armed him with the authority to exercise the powers of the Presidency.

President Jonathan realises the dilemma confronting his ambition, hence his contention that it would be better to be president for nine years than eight years. Had the Nigerian constitution borrowed from the American prescriptions in presidential succession politics, the dilemma facing Jonathan would not have been there. Were he to be in a position to contest the Presidency in 2015, a successful Jonathan would not only have taken the oath of office three times, but would also have been President for nine years by 2019. It would be interesting to know how the 1999 constitution would be negotiated or navigated.

Following the 22nd amendment which limited the American president to two terms in office, its drafters made provision for a president who could be taking over from one who was unable to complete his or her term of office. The maximum number of years one can be president of the United States of America was pegged at 10. This means the eligibility of a succeeding president to seek re-election, after he or she might have won a term of their own, would always depend on when he or she ascended into the presidency.

Lyndon Johnson, who ascended the American Presidency in a circumstance similar to that of our own President Jonathan, was eminently qualified to seek re-election in 1968, not least because another four years in office would mean he was president for only nine years. Johnson succeeded the assassinated John Kennedy in 1963, won an election of his own in 1964, but chose not to seek re-election in 1968 for personal reasons. Of course, taking over from a president who did not complete his or her tenure could, in the American context, also mean that a succeeding president was limited to barely six years in office. It is always a matter of how far the presidency of one has advanced before another took over.

Aside from the constitutional clog in the ambition of Jonathan, there is this temptation for one to believe he might have actually agreed with others that he would not be seeking re-election in 2015. One is tempted to subscribe to this view on the evidence of the controversy surrounding his candidacy in the 2011 election. With the contention over zoning or no zoning in the Peoples Democratic Party, those who canvassed support for Jonathan said he was completing the mandate he jointly held with the late Yar'Adua. Even when the veracity of that argument could easily have been debunked, it was one argument in political expediency that has now become a moral burden for Jonathan.

*Punch, 18 August 2014*

## Lessons From US Presidential Term Limits

Political sycophants abound everywhere and would seem to be products of a nation's stage of historical development. Even when it should be a personal decision whether or not one runs for office, there may have been sycophants in Nigeria vowing to divorce their wives or husbands if President Goodluck Jonathan did not re-contest the presidency in 2015.

Similarly, at the early stages of American political history, there were said to be sycophants who urged George Washington, America's first president from 1789-1797, to transform himself into being the first King of America in the tradition of colonial Britain. Washington was said to have reminded his fellow Americans that it was because of the tyranny of the British monarch that they fought a war of Independence in 1776. Against the pressure of others, Washington did not re-contest the presidency after he had served two terms in office.

Principally, because of Washington's voluntary withdrawal, it was always assumed that the American president was conventionally limited to two terms in office. Their Constitution of 1787 did not state how long one could be President of the United States.

However, what seemed to have been the convention in American politics changed in 1940 when Franklin Delano Roosevelt won a third election to the presidency. He was a highly successful president who had steered his nation through the Great Depression of the 1930s. He, in fact, was elected in 1944 for a fourth term which he did not complete. He died in 1945.

Be that as it may, Republicans in Congress sought passage of an amendment that would limit the terms of future presidents. FDR was the first and only American president to serve more than two terms in office. The term limits are, however, made clear in the following words:

*"Passed by Congress in 1947, and ratified by the states on February 27, 1951, the Twenty-Second Amendment limits an elected president to two terms in office, a*

230

*total of eight years. However, it is possible for an individual to serve up to 10 years as president. The amendment specifies that if a vice-president or other successor takes over from a president – who, for whatever reason, cannot fulfil the term – and serves two years or less of the former president's term, the new president may serve for two full four-year terms. If more than two years remain of the term when the successor assumes office, the new President may serve only one additional term."*

Lyndon Johnson, as highlighted in a previous article, was qualified to seek a second four-year term in 1968. However, Gerald Ford who was president from 1974 to 1977, having succeeded the impeached Richard Nixon, would only have qualified to contest the 1976 election which he did contest and lost to Jimmy Carter. Ford served more than two years of the "unexpired" term of Nixon.

What relevance has the Twenty-Second Amendment to our situation in Nigeria? One has tried to explain this for the simple reason that it could serve as a guide for the eligibility of President Jonathan, whose route to the Presidency began via succession rather than election, to contest the Nigerian 2015 election.

The American Twenty-Second Amendment tells us that it does matter that one has ascended the presidency, even when he or she was not the one elected into that position. In the eyes of that Amendment, less than two years of the term of another may not be long enough to constitute one term in the entitlement of a succeeding president. In which case, Jonathan's re-election in 2015 would not have been the constitutional issue it currently is, had we borrowed from the wisdom of America's Twenty-Second Amendment. Jonathan had served less than two years of the unexpired term of his deceased predecessor in office.

However, in spite of the pollution of the democratic space by the noises of those begging Jonathan to contest the 2015 presidential election- state-sponsored sycophancy, some would say- the man himself has said only the national interest would determine whether or not he would be doing so. What constitutes the national interest could be subjective here.

*Punch, 13 October 2014*

# A Rejection of Dodgy "Transformation"

The culture of wanting to induce the support of potential voters with gifts dates back to the introduction of electoral politics in our polity. One had observed, while growing up as a child, that politicians of the First Republic gave bags of salt to voting communities in anticipation of their support. In my community, potential voters considered it a taboo to accept salt from a candidate they would not be voting for. Even when seeking to induce support with a gift of any nature, as well as accepting it, should be considered wrong, Nigerians of a generation did demonstrate somehow that they had honour and integrity.

This can hardly be said of Nigerians of today; there are not a few who have been "groomed" into anticipating that they must be bribed by whoever was seeking their support. It has also become something akin to an official policy – stomach infrastructure – to seek to corrupt the sensibilities of would-be voters with gifts that are merely periodic – gifts at election time by politicians who would not give a damn about the plight of ordinary Nigerians once their motives have been achieved.

Of course, ours is still a very crude democracy but the need for a change of attitude cannot be more urgent. In the advanced democratic nations of the world, it would be against the law of the land to offer or accept bribes for the purpose of procuring electoral support. Politicians of enlightened societies "bribe" with their manifestos. At every election year, the potential voter is able to judge for himself or herself if politicians have been faithful to their promises. Without any sentiment, primordial or otherwise, the voting public would ask those seeking their support, especially for re-election: "Are we better off today than we were four or five years ago when we first elected you into office?" How one wishes our Nigerian voters had matured to this level!

I was not one of the most enthusiastic advocates of the Goodluck Jonathan Presidency in the 2011 election, not least because of my honest support for the principle of rotational presidency. However, I had wished President Jonathan would succeed with his philosophy of "transformation". Transformation, in my honest assumption, should not just be about changing or improving the physical landscape of society; the transformation that can endure should be one that has resulted in bringing about attitudinal changes that conform to acceptable standards of decency and civilised behaviour.

There are a few things one wished Jonathan had done differently if he were a transforming President. If he was constitutionally qualified to seek re-election, and he believed he had done reasonably well as President, why pretend to Nigerians about his ambition to want to continue in office? Why would a successful leader have unleashed on our streets a hoard of sycophants, apparently at the expense of our common purse, to engage in the nuisance of having to be begging him to seek re-election?

There were those who more or less vowed to divorce their wives if the "greatest president on earth", some kind of "Jesus Christ", did not listen to their prayers and seek re-election in 2015. Suddenly, the reluctant Jonathan emerged as the sole candidate of his party, having scared away potential rivals from the contest!

There is also this allegation that "Ghana-must-go" sacks of assorted currencies were ferried into the homes of influential Nigerians – traditional rulers, pastors, and Imams, among others. There would appear to have consequently been a flurry of endorsements, even by those who should know better that wanting to put a new constitution in place would require the co-operation of all major political parties and not just the promise of an individual.

Finally, there is this serious allegation of military complicity in the outcome of the Ekiti State governorship election of June 2014. It was a verifiable allegation made by an identifiable commissioned officer of the Nigerian Army. He would not have taken a risk on his life and career if he was not convinced of what he had observed and felt disturbed by it.

*The Guardian, 04 March 2015*

# The Democracy of Anarchists

UNTIL the introduction of foreign religions, Ifa (the God of divination) solely provided spiritual guidance in the Yoruba traditional setting. Whenever the Ifa was consulted and it revealed a potential problem, the priest or priestess would "enquire" if there was a remedy or whatever could be done to mitigate the eventuality of the problem foreseen.

There were always problems and there would always be problems; the most important thing is for us not to be consumed by the problems that come our way. An American Think Tank, as far back as 2005, projected a disturbing scenario for our nation in this very year of 2015. Their report did not state categorically that our nation would disintegrate. However, it highlighted a possible intervention in politics by a junior military officer with all its attendant consequences. Many Nigerians, including this writer, did not reflect at that time that 2015 would be an election year. There were vitriolic attacks on the report and the evil intentions of its authors pontificated on the pages of newspapers.

There were hardly any debates in Nigeria, either by politicians or the intelligentsia, on a report that projects so much danger for our nation. Of course, our nation has potential to be great; the truth of world politics is that the powerful nations of the world do not deliberately welcome new members into their fold! Be that as it may, elections in Nigeria have historically been problematic. The mismanaged federal elections of 1964, as well as those in the Western Region in 1965, resulted in the collapse of the First Republic on January 15, 1966.

The aftermath was a war fought between 1967 and 1970. Similarly, mismanaged elections in 1983 led to the military coup of December that year. Although the politicians of today, for opportunistic reasons, would want to vilify those who staged the coup in their usual rhetoric, the fact remains that we were all on the streets celebrating the overthrow of a most corrupt and insensitive collection of politicians.

The late J.M. Johnson, a most flamboyant politician of the First Republic, prayed never again to witness "democracy" in his lifetime. Chief Arthur Nzeribe, himself a politician of the Second Republic, organised a rally in London in support of the new military messiahs. Post Second Republic elections have hardly revealed any improvements or progress in our democratic journey. The annulled presidential election of June 1993 led to a crisis that threatened the foundations of our society. The military approach to governance, especially during the irrational dictatorship of kleptocratic and profligate Sani Abacha, resulted in the rise of various ethnic militias.

These anarchic militias have yet to disappear and today's politicians would seem to have resuscitated their venom for opportunistic purposes. A history of ugly elections makes the fear of what we now call "American prediction", very real. We hardly need the Ifa priest to warn us of where our problem could be coming from – the defining elections of 2015. This writer has said it repeatedly in articles, that there comes a time in the life of a nation when an individual could redirect the course of a dangerous history by sacrificing his or her ambition for the greater good. Given the circumstances of our contemporary history, one had thought we could navigate the terrains of political danger were Goodluck Jonathan to have supervised the 2015 elections, rather than be a participant.

Since he has an "ambition" to protect, the realistic phase of our advice would now be to continue to warn against "desperation", not only on his part but also on the part of his major rival, General Muhammadu Buhari of the All Progressives Congress (APC). There have been all sorts of dangerous propaganda and insinuations here and there but the most disturbing chapter of political desperation has revealed itself in the deployment of ethnic militias to argue the case of a particular political party with threats of violence.

There is hardly any doubt that the "Jega must go" protests by the Movement for the Actualization of the Sovereign State of Biafra

(MASSOB) and the Oodua Peoples Congress (OPC), in the South East and South West respectively, were sponsored by vested political interests. These irredentist and somewhat anarchic tendencies would undoubtedly troop into the streets soon after the elections to unleash terror, especially if the outcome did not favour their privileged sponsors.

The history of our nation reveals that the politicians themselves would be the greatest losers were the democratic process to be terminated again. However, our more urgent concern here is with ordinary Nigerians. We are concerned that the desperation of a tiny class of corrupt and undemocratic politicians could be the cause of "mass graves" for innocent citizens; may God forbid!!!

*The Guardian, 20 March 2015*

# Odds in Favour of Buhari

The one picture you would hate to see in your dreams is that of the very opponent of the team you are supporting, clutching a massive trophy and jubilating all over the place! Not just once had one experienced a 'nightmarish' dream of this nature and not just once had 'Joseph the Octopus' proved to be revealing exactly what was about to happen.

Of course, it should not be interpreted as if one does not want Maj. Gen. Muhammadu Buhari to be the next president of the Federal Republic of Nigeria but what the hell was he doing in my dream smiling so broadly as he acknowledged shouts of 'congratulations' from a horde of adoring supporters? The man can hardly manage a smile in real life and neither is he the candidate one would ordinarily be rooting for. However, a warning would seem to have come from the unknown: 'Do not bet your house against Buhari becoming (the next) president unless you are equally prepared to be homeless!"

The above extracts are from an article I wrote (title retained) in the run-up to the 2011 presidential election, having dreamt that Maj. Gen Muhammadu Buhari won the election. Of course, he did not but, who knows, it could have been a distant event that one had foreseen!

In trying to rationalise the circumstances that could have made it a dream-come-true for Buhari, I examined the controversy that surrounded the candidacy of President Goodluck Jonathan over the zoning philosophy of his party, the Peoples Democratic Party. That controversy, more or less, pitted the northern leadership against him. I also examined the possibility that the then so-called progressive parties might actually co-operate among themselves in order to counterbalance the influence and power of the PDP. An attempt made in that direction did not succeed.

Quite a lot has changed since 2011 and the aforementioned factors, more than ever before, will have implications for the direction of the Presidency come February 14.

Firstly, the once splinter progressive parties have coalesced into the All Progressives Congress, thanks to the centralising influence of the institution of the Presidency. The February presidential election will be fought in what is a two-party competition between the PDP and the APC. Buhari could be the beneficiary of this new development, as he now competes for the Presidency under the platform of a political party which, unlike his defunct Congress for Political Change, enjoys nationwide support.

Secondly, the February elections will reveal the extent to which the intra-party crisis in the PDP – a crisis which led to the defection of five of its governors to the rival APC – has resulted into the loss or gain of popular support in the various constituencies. I have attempted to explain the causes of the crisis in the PDP by three factors: "One, a frosty relationship between President Goodluck Jonathan and Governor Rotimi Amaechi of Rivers State; two, an allegation of arbitrariness on the part of the immediate past PDP national chairman, Alhaji Bamanga Tukur; and three, the perceived ambition of President Jonathan to seek re-election in 2015 in contradiction of a supposed agreement that he would not be doing so." (see my book, Party Coalitions in Nigeria (2014), pp. 129-130).

Cleavage, be it of ethnicity or religion, is the worst of political problems. You hardly can resolve the problem of cleavage by preaching to people to forget about those things they hold very dear to their hearts. There are not a few in the North who feel the South had dominated the Presidency for the greater part of the current Republic; they will grab the opportunity provided by the candidacy of Muhammadu Buhari in ensuring that the pendulum of political power swings back to their region.

Finally, Buhari faces an incumbent President, Goodluck Jonathan, who may be having problems with economic and security issues.

Allegations of escalating official corruption and Boko Haram insurgency in the North-East may have overshadowed the modest achievements of Jonathan. Of course, diverse sentiments will compete and contend in the 2015 election, but there are not a few who would want to reward or punish him on their perception of his stewardship during the past four years. Buhari, himself a former leader, has his own "baggages" but he enjoys the perception of being one disciplined individual who passionately resents corruption. Corruption has been that most deadly virus afflicting the Nigerian state.

There is hardly any doubt that the days ahead will be quite interesting. What we must continue to do is to educate our people about the ramifications of democracy as a game where the minority must have its say while the majority has its way. Why, for instance, would you want to throw the nation into chaos just because someone has lost an election, even when another member of your ethnic or religious constituency could be a beneficiary in the near future? Why would you want the stigma of "intolerant democrats" stamped permanently on you and your people? Our nation must unite behind whoever wins the February presidential election.

*Punch, 23 January 2015*

# Buhari Deserves a Smile

The political parties of our borrowed presidential system are not opposing parties in the context of adversarial politics. Political parties of American- style democracy are programmed to be able to work together. Even when a political party does not control the Executive arm of government, it plays a major part in the Legislature. The concept of "opposition leader" or "opposition party" hardly exists in American political discourse or literature. That concept belongs in the Westminster-style democracy which we discarded in the First Republic.

Hopefully, we will be able to sustain our democracy and improve on its culture. One hopes for a future when our political parties would have matured and developed individual characters and Nigerians simply refer to two major divides as "The Progressives" and "The Democrats", or whatever. The political party is a product of its environment; the quality of our political parties will always be a reflection of our collective advancements in all spheres of human endeavour.

The recently concluded presidential election has its own significance, being the first election in the history of Nigeria in which an incumbent President was defeated in an election that was relatively free and fair. President Goodluck Jonathan, even when some might have reservations about his electioneering style and pronouncements, did play the part of a gallant sportsman by conceding victory to his opponent, Muhammadu Buhari (now President-elect), in an admired democratic manner. That symbolic gesture of his can only be rubbished by the Orubebes threatening to challenge a clear and predictable victory in the tribunals. President Jonathan has played a gallant role in the democratic process and should not be a part of that joke.

The essence of periodic elections is to afford the voting public an opportunity to decide on who governs them from time to time. It is also a warning to the ruling elite that the public must not be taken for granted. Defeat at the polls provides the leadership of the affected political party an opportunity to regroup, re-assess strategies, and plot its way back in a future election. And, of course, the victorious party must not over-celebrate because it does not take long before the political music changes.

One cannot but congratulate the man of the moment, Buhari, on a well-deserved victory. Musician Jimmy Cliff must have had him in mind when he wrote his song, "You can get it if you really want". Not many would have been as dogged as he was on the campaign trail since 2003, pursuing an ambition or an aspiration. There is hardly any doubt that the man has an ambition to make a positive mark on history and we pray with him that he succeeds in the interest of all of us. Buhari was our leader between December 1983 and August 1985. We had cause to celebrate him then, and we also had cause to chastise him. He has matured with age, and he has had decades to reflect on things.He must prove his admirers right, and his doubters wrong. He owes that to himself, the nation, and history.

Buhari should know that Nigerians are in a hurry to see results. His mission to rescue Nigeria must begin in earnest. He needs our co-operation and goodwill. He needs the support of those who, along with him, have been elected into the legislative arm of government. In tune with the realities of contemporary Nigeria, our demand to these individuals is to trim their excesses. The salaries and allowances they corner to themselves do not portray them as a class of politicians who mean well for the future. They must be reminded that they are lawmakers and their so-called constituency allowances cannot exceed what they need to maintain administrative offices. We have not elected them for the purpose of distributing goodies to friends and political associates. The voters must also be educated about the limits of the functions of those they have elected into various offices

Please, do this for us Buhari — sell off some of the presidential jets as a message to the Nigerian public that the war against corruption and official profligacy has returned to our shores!

*The Guardian, 03 April 2015*

## Of Defections and Political Prostitution

One major difference in the politics of the advanced democratic nations and that of contemporary Nigeria is that one is highly 'individualistic' while the other is still largely 'communal'. By this I mean there is a greater degree of independence in one than exists in the other. Whereas the divorce lawyer may not be summoned because a wife has chosen to hold a political view that is different from that of her husband, this may not be the case in a communal society where the choice made by one person could be taken, invariably, as the choice made by others. It is precisely because of this communal culture that the phenomenon of defections, i.e. crossing over from one political party to another, attracts the attention it hardly deserves.

When a key political actor has defected from one political party to another, there is a 'bandwagon' effect helped by a very low level of political education as well as economic poverty on the part of others. I remember when my father, the late Chief Josiah Akinola Oisa was 'coerced' into transferring his loyalty from the National Council of Nigeria and the Cameroons (NCNC) in the late 1950s, quite a number of erstwhile supporters of the party followed him to the ruling Action Group (AG) in the then Western Region.

He was quite an influential chief, very intelligent as he was equally principled and bold. However, the 'regional government' threatened him with deposition if he did not switch loyalty. Deposition was, and still is, some kind of disgrace no one would wish for. My father reluctantly abandoned the political party he so much cherished, thanks to the intolerance of those in positions of power and authority. He was not given the option of being paid 'a penny a year salary'.

Armed with what I observed as a very young child, I took exceptional interest in the phenomenon of defections during the Second Republic (1979-83). I was about arguing a thesis that the presidency would bring about a two-party system in Nigeria, hence the excitement in an observation that members of minor political parties were defecting in large numbers to the then two relatively successful parties, the National Party of Nigeria (NPN) and the Unity Party of Nigeria (UPN). I saw the development as a process of 'party cross-breeding'. The termination of the then democratic experiment, not least because of the culture of election rigging, frustrated whatever outcome or conclusion one was anticipating.

There have been quite a few noticeable defections since political party activity resumed in 1999; however, the phenomenon of defections has never been as pronounced as it has been in the past couple of months. The internal crisis in the ruling Peoples Democratic Party (PDP) opened up a floodgate of defections, with as many as five governors as well as Senators and Representatives transferring their loyalty from the PDP to the new alternative political party, the All Progressives Congress (APC). Of course, the PDP has equally been benefiting from the spate of defections as well as allegedly 'buying back' its fleeing members.

The ease with which our politicians change political party support clearly suggests that ideology is of little relevance in our politics. Our politicians are divided by their greed and selfish interests than by anything else. Where there is commitment to ideology, a politician will not transfer his or her loyalty for the fear of competition by potential rivals. They will not be running from the political party they believed in for the fear that its structure could be hijacked by another. On the contrary, an ideologically-informed politician will remain in his or her party and sort out whatever problems might have arisen.

It will take quite a while for the Nigerian party system to stabilize. The party system is evolving, still some kind of work in progress. The one good thing to take from current observations is the potential for integration being exhibited by the presidency as a political institution. There will be those arguing for Nigeria to return to the parliamentary system of government which was practiced in the First Republic, not least because it is believed to be less expensive than the presidential alternative.

However, when it comes to the issue of political integration, I shall be one of those arguing that the presidential system should be accepted as having come to stay. A return to the parliamentary system will be a return to another era of ethnic political parties and the erstwhile culture of conspiratorial ethnic alliances.

There is nothing to be nostalgic about in the practice of the parliamentary system as witnessed at the federal level of political governance until its deserved death on 15 January 1966. The emergence of the PDP and the APC, as broad-based political parties, has revealed the centralizing influence of the presidency and proved beyond reasonable doubt that there is no place for ethnic political parties in the current dispensation.

A bit of tinkering with the constitution, especially at the level of leadership recruitment (rotating the presidency, for instance) could tame the spate of defections and political prostitution

*Punch, 19 February 2014*